BALTIMORE

A DRAMA BY

Kirsten Greenidge

Baltimore (1st ed. - 02.24.16) - baltimore7lm
Copyright © 2016 Kirsten Greenidge

ALL RIGHTS RESERVED

Copyright Protection. This play (the "Play") is fully protected under the copyright laws of the United States of America and all countries with which the United States has reciprocal copyright relations, whether through bilateral or multilateral treaties or otherwise, and including, but not limited to, all countries covered by the Pan-American Copyright Convention, the Universal Copyright Convention, and the Berne Convention.

Reservation of Rights. All rights to this Play are strictly reserved, including, without limitation, professional and amateur stage performance rights; motion picture, recitation, lecturing, public reading, radio broadcasting, television, video, and sound recording rights; rights to all other forms of mechanical or electronic reproduction now known or yet to be invented, such as CD-ROM, CD-I, DVD, photocopying, and information storage and retrieval systems; and the rights of translation into non-English languages.

Performance Licensing and Royalty Payments. Amateur and stock performance rights to this Play are controlled exclusively by Playscripts, Inc. ("Playscripts"). No amateur or stock production groups or individuals may perform this Play without obtaining advance written permission from Playscripts. Required royalty fees for performing this Play are specified online at the Playscripts website (www.playscripts.com). Such royalty fees may be subject to change without notice. Although this book may have been obtained for a particular licensed performance, such performance rights, if any, are not transferable. Required royalties must be paid every time the Play is performed before any audience, whether or not it is presented for profit and whether or not admission is charged. All licensing requests and inquiries concerning amateur and stock performance rights should be addressed to Playscripts (see contact information on opposite page).

Inquiries concerning all other rights should be addressed to the author's agent: Bruce Ostler, Bret Adams, Ltd, 448 West 44th Street, New York, NY, 10036.

Restriction of Alterations. There shall be no deletions, alterations, or changes of any kind made to the Play, including the changing of character gender, the cutting of dialogue, the cutting of music, or the alteration of objectionable language, unless directly authorized by Playscripts. The title of the Play shall not be altered.

Author Credit. Any individual or group receiving permission to produce this Play is required to give credit to the author as the sole and exclusive author of the Play. This obligation applies to the title page of every program distributed in connection with performances of the Play, and in any instance that the title of the Play appears for purposes of advertising, publicizing, or otherwise exploiting the Play and/or a production thereof. The name of the author must appear on a separate line, in which no other name appears, immediately beneath the title and of a font size at least 50% as large as the largest letter used in the title of the Play. No person, firm, or entity may receive credit larger or more prominent than that accorded the author. The name of the author may not be abbreviated or otherwise altered from the form in which it appears in this Play.

Publisher Attribution. All programs, advertisements, and other printed material distributed or published in connection with the amateur or stock production of the Play shall include the following notice:

Produced by special arrangement with Playscripts, Inc.
(www.playscripts.com)

Prohibition of Unauthorized Copying. Any unauthorized copying of this book or excerpts from this book is strictly forbidden by law. Except as otherwise permitted by applicable law, no part of this book may be reproduced, stored in a retrieval system, or transmitted in any form, by any means now known or yet to be invented, including, without limitation, photocopying or scanning, without prior permission from Playscripts.

Statement of Non-affiliation. This Play may include references to brand names and trademarks owned by third parties, and may include references to public figures. Playscripts is not necessarily affiliated with these public figures, or with the owners of such trademarks and brand names. Such references are included solely for parody, political comment, or other permitted purposes.

Permissions for Sound Recordings and Musical Works. This Play may contain directions calling for the performance of a portion, or all, of a musical work *not included in the Play's score*, or performance of a sound recording of such a musical work. Playscripts has not obtained permissions to perform such works. The producer of this Play is advised to obtain such permissions, if required in the context of the production. The producer is directed to the websites of the U.S. Copyright Office (www.copyright.gov), ASCAP (www.ascap.com), BMI (www.bmi.com), and NMPA (www.nmpa.org) for further information on the need to obtain permissions, and on procedures for obtaining such permissions.

The Rules in Brief

1) Do NOT perform this Play without obtaining prior permission from Playscripts, and without paying the required royalty.
2) Do NOT photocopy, scan, or otherwise duplicate any part of this book.
3) Do NOT alter the text of the Play, change a character's gender, delete any dialogue, cut any music, or alter any objectionable language, unless explicitly authorized by Playscripts.
4) DO provide the required credit to the author(s) and the required attribution to Playscripts in all programs and promotional literature associated with any performance of this Play.

For more details on these and other rules, see the opposite page.

Copyright Basics

This Play is protected by United States and international copyright law. These laws ensure that authors are rewarded for creating new and vital dramatic work, and protect them against theft and abuse of their work.

A play is a piece of property, fully owned by the author, just like a house or car. You must obtain permission to use this property, and must pay a royalty fee for the privilege—whether or not you charge an admission fee. Playscripts collects these required payments on behalf of the author.

Anyone who violates an author's copyright is liable as a copyright infringer under United States and international law. Playscripts and the author are entitled to institute legal action for any such infringement, which can subject the infringer to actual damages, statutory damages, and attorneys' fees. A court may impose statutory damages of up to $150,000 for willful copyright infringements. U.S. copyright law also provides for possible criminal sanctions. Visit the website of the U.S. Copyright Office (www.copyright.gov) for more information.

THE BOTTOM LINE: If you break copyright law, you are robbing a playwright and opening yourself to expensive legal action. Follow the rules, and when in doubt, ask us.

Playscripts, Inc.
7 Penn Plaza, Suite 904
New York, NY 10001

toll-free phone: 1-866-NEW-PLAY
email: info@playscripts.com
website: www.playscripts.com

Cast of Characters

SHELBY, 20, African American, resident advisor, sheltered upbringing but outspoken, naïve despite her many academic and extracurricular achievements, female.

ALYSSA, 18, of color, one of Shelby's residents on the floor, smart, female.

FIONA, 18, white, American, one of Shelby's residents on the floor. Also smart, loves pranks, female.

RACHEL, 18, American, Latina. Also identifies as being a Latina with light skin, one of Shelby's residents on the floor. Smart. Socially conscious, perhaps overtly so, female.

LEIGH, 18, of color, American, one of Shelby's residents on the floor, female.

BRYANT, 18, of color, American, one of Shelby's residents, male.

CARSON, 18, white, American, one of Shelby's residents, male.

GRACE, 20, Shelby's friend, lives off-campus, Asian American.

DEAN HERNANDEZ, 50s, of color, black and Latino male.*

**It is not essential Dean Hernandez be played by an actor who is actually in his 50s.*

Setting

The dean's office; a campus bench; a common room on a dormitory floor on the campus of a small New England college.

Time

The present.

All action takes place over a twelve-hour period, between the afternoon and sunrise.

Casting Notes

In regard to casting and race: race and how it is represented and discussed in the text as it refers to the actors chosen can and should be fluid. For example, as written, there are references to Rachel identifying as a Latina (i.e. her family and ancestors are from Spanish-speaking countries in North, Central, and/or South America / Latin America and the Caribbean Islands), not Hispanic, and when people see her they do not identify her as Latina. If the actor playing Rachel has traits that seem to identify her as being Latina, it is okay to slightly modify text to reflect this. To verify these text changes, please contact the author's publisher and/or agent before public presentation.

It is essential that the actor playing Grace feel comfortable in this role. Please contact the playwright via the publisher for a modified script if the actor playing Grace is not Korean American and would like access to a script that honors another ethnicity.

Please contact the playwright for similar concerns about the other roles. Otherwise, please cast according to the ethnicity specified for each character.

Acknowledgments

Baltimore was commissioned by the Big Ten Theatre Consortium as part of an initiative to support new plays by women with major roles for female actors.

Many thanks to the following for their help and guidance in the writing and development of *Baltimore*: Naomi Iizuka; Leslie Felbain, Leigh Smiley, and the students at the University of Maryland's Department of Theatre and Dance; New Repertory's Next Voices; Elaine Van Houge and the students at the School of Theatre at Boston University; Rhombus; Alan MacVey, Aislinn Franz, and Mark Orsini.

BALTIMORE
by Kirsten Greenidge

(A large projection in the shape of a dry erase board overhead.
As house lights lower we hear the sound of dry erase marker on dry erase board.
Squeak, squeak, squeak.
The black outline of an open book appears on the dry erase board. First the book cover, then the open pages. On the spine the words: "study break" appear in fun, bubbly lettering.
House lights down.)

(Lights up fully on stage.
The dean's office.
Afternoon.
If there is a realized set, then there should be moving boxes scattered around the office.
SHELBY *stands, smartphone in hand.*
DEAN HERNANDEZ *sits.*
SHELBY *seems to be having trouble with said smartphone.*
The sound of a cymbal—crisp.)

DEAN HERNANDEZ. ...So really, my hope is to help foster that here, on our own campus. Because really, when we say community, my query is: what do we actually—

SHELBY. Hold on. I'm sorry.

DEAN HERNANDEZ. No, no, of course.

SHELBY. New phone.

DEAN HERNANDEZ. Ah.

(A ring tone.)

SHELBY. Shit.

*(*SHELBY *looks up at* DEAN HERNANDEZ.*)*

SHELBY. I mean shoot.

*(*DEAN HERNANDEZ *smiles.)*

SHELBY. Sorry, Dean Hernandez, I'm so sorry.

DEAN HERNANDEZ. The turnip truck didn't just drop me off, Miss Wilson. I've heard a few salty words in my time.

*(*SHELBY *seems to freeze, looks at* DEAN HERNANDEZ.*)*

DEAN HERNANDEZ. Yours aren't the first.

SHELBY. Oh right, right. Okay, so, where were…togetherness, together, all together–

DEAN HERNANDEZ. Community.

(Ring tone.)

SHELBY. Keep talking, I'm getting all this.

*(*DEAN HERNANDEZ *goes to speak–*
Ring tone.)

SHELBY. Damn it.

(Ring.
SHELBY *looks at* DEAN HERNANDEZ.*)*

SHELBY. I mean–

DEAN HERNANDEZ. Perhaps you should pick up.

SHELBY. It's really nothing.

(Ring.
SHELBY *turns her ringer off.)*

SHELBY. See? Keep going. Union, union…

(The phone vibrates.)

DEAN HERNANDEZ. Pick up, if you need to, Miss Wilson.

(The phone vibrates.
SHELBY *fiddles with her phone some more.*
She settles herself.
She focuses on DEAN HERNANDEZ*.)*

SHELBY. Unity. Got it. Go ahead.

(The phone beeps.)

DEAN HERNANDEZ. Maybe it's your father–

*(*SHELBY *shakes her head "no.")*

DEAN HERNANDEZ. Your mother–

SHELBY. No, no, she, they, know I have this interview. With you. They know not to call.

(Ring tone.
SHELBY *presses her phone.)*

SHELBY. I just need the recorder to–

(Text notification sounds.)

DEAN HERNANDEZ. Perhaps Miss Haj can help you to reschedule—

SHELBY. No no no, Dean Hernandez, I can finish, we can— I'd turn the whole thing off but I need the recorder to—

(The phone makes a curious bleeping noise.
SHELBY *looks down at the phone.)*

DEAN HERNANDEZ. Miss Haj keeps my book. She can reschedule.

SHELBY. This interview, your interview is due tomorrow, though, Dean Hernandez, and I. I mean it's an important piece. About your coming to SU, Sudbury, your starting here. The first black dean in, in—

DEAN HERNANDEZ. Ever.

SHELBY. Right, yes, so it's important.

DEAN HERNANDEZ. Well thank you.

SHELBY. And what you have to say. About. About. I mean there's here but out. Beyond Sudbury, your work. Is. Crucial. I know my parents think so. I mean I think so too. I do. I agree. I AGREE.

DEAN HERNANDEZ. With what, Miss Wilson?

*(*SHELBY *looks at* DEAN HERNANDEZ.
DEAN HERNANDEZ *looks at* SHELBY.
SHELBY *seems to brace herself, then:)*

SHELBY. And it's due at eight AM so maybe this can just be a conversation?

(The phone makes a whirring sound.
SHELBY *looks down at her phone.*
DEAN HERNANDEZ *chuckles.*
SHELBY *regroups.)*

SHELBY. I'll turn my phone off and we can just talk.

DEAN HERNANDEZ. The old-fashioned way.

SHELBY. Great. Excellent.

*(*SHELBY *puts her phone away.)*

DEAN HERNANDEZ. So let's: *converse.*

*(*DEAN HERNANDEZ *grins.)*

SHELBY. Or. Well. Um how about you just, you could just talk?

DEAN HERNANDEZ. You do not have any questions?

SHELBY. Sure I do. Of course I do.

(Beat.
DEAN HERNANDEZ *looks at* SHELBY.
SHELBY *looks at* DEAN HERNANDEZ.
SHELBY *grins sheepishly.)*

DEAN HERNANDEZ. And so, what are these questions, Miss Wilson?

SHELBY. I'm, I'm really lost without my phone. My. Questions are on my phone.

DEAN HERNANDEZ. I see.

SHELBY. But we can do this. I can do this. What, what would you like to—

DEAN HERNANDEZ. That is the point, Miss Wilson, what is it *you* would like to know?

SHELBY. Well um. How about all that stuff you said last week when school started, at convocation, about leadership and, and, what you said about the civic, the civic, ins…insti—

DEAN HERNANDEZ. Impulse—

SHELBY. Yeah, right. That is so interesting. That is so important.

DEAN HERNANDEZ. Oh, I am so glad to hear you attended convocation. Not many students, especially you juniors and seniors, I've found, take the time to attend, to listen and attend. Interesting word "attend": to be *present, to show up.* So, that's, well that's a fine place to start, don't you agree? Tell me—I'm very interested—what did you think of the convocation?

(SHELBY *looks at* DEAN HERNANDEZ.
SHELBY *blinks.*
SHELBY *gulps.)*

SHELBY. Well we, the *Sentinel*—

DEAN HERNANDEZ. The university's journal—

SHELBY. Newspaper. I'm assistant editor, sort of, I mean I could be. This article could help me to be, by the end of the semester anyway. Anyway, yeah. The *Sentinel* posted online—

DEAN HERNANDEZ. You just never know who is out there. I'm so glad to know—

SHELBY. Well, yeah, right, they, we— The university makes the first years go to that kind of stuff, but I'm a junior, I mean, I— See, you see, I'm an RA this semester, this year, this whole year, and that takes up, took up, it takes up so much— There's this one girl who keeps, she's like homesick? I think? And I was, she, her parents, her mom, I was on the phone, like in California there's the time difference and I was– The night before convocation this mom would not– It was like this long phone call that would not: *stop*: did not *end*—and it's like: your daughter's eigh*teen,* she is *fine*—but this *phone* call would not *stop* this mom was like a wind-up toy or something and, and, I had to you know like calm down like de-stress and re-group after all that so um I went out and I know I shouldn't've but I really, was just so stressed really stressed out I mean completely exhausted so I had to get my mind off it, you know? Margarita Mondays: Sunset Cantina: 5.99. Mango. But I. That means I. Totally slept through my alarm. My phone is possessed—you see how it's possessed– I totally slept through convocation, through your welcome speech at convocation—but I read it online most of it online and I have to say I really. Yeah. Enjoyed it.

(DEAN HERNANDEZ *smiles.)*

DEAN HERNANDEZ. Enjoyed it.

SHELBY. I did.

DEAN HERNANDEZ. Which parts, precisely, did you enjoy?

(SHELBY *looks at* DEAN HERNANDEZ.
DEAN HERNANDEZ *smiles at* SHELBY.)

SHELBY. Well. I.

(SHELBY *looks at* DEAN HERNANDEZ.)

DEAN HERNANDEZ. *Ah.*

SHELBY. No, no, I read it.

DEAN HERNANDEZ. The present evidence points to the contrary, Miss Wilson.

SHELBY. I did. I read it, I mean. Well. Actually. I've found. That. If I read each line of a long story or, right, like article I just. It takes so much. Time.

DEAN HERNANDEZ. It does yes.

SHELBY. So I skim. I taught myself to be efficient. With my time. I *skim.* I totally got everything you were saying, though.

DEAN HERNANDEZ. You're making me think I should have accepted the offer from State.

SHELBY. I did. I read it. I really did.

DEAN HERNANDEZ. Make me sleep easy I chose the right student body, Miss Wilson.

SHELBY. I just didn't. Agree with it.

DEAN HERNANDEZ. Okay. All right. Now we're cooking, right?

(SHELBY *looks at* DEAN HERNANDEZ.)

SHELBY. I mean.

(SHELBY *looks at* DEAN HERNANDEZ.)

SHELBY. I mean you talk about people like they're, we're vegetables, fruits and vegetables at the grocery store. You know, with barcodes or something.

DEAN HERNANDEZ. We each meet each other with a certain history lapping at our insides.

(SHELBY *looks at* DEAN HERNANDEZ.
SHELBY *blinks.*)

SHELBY. But labels like that are kind of. I don't like labels very much. We're all human, right? I told that to my floor their first day and they really got it, I think. Your speech. Kind of. Made me feel. A little bad about myself. The world's different now. People my age, need, need–

DEAN HERNANDEZ. Better answers.

SHELBY. Our world is much more complex, much more, much more–

DEAN HERNANDEZ. So why bother speaking out, fighting at all–

SHELBY. No, I–

DEAN HERNANDEZ. Or maybe the fight is over. Maybe everyone just needs an iPhone and a good job.

SHELBY. Mad respect, for your work, for like what you write about, about consciousness–

DEAN HERNANDEZ. Awakening.

(SHELBY *looks at* DEAN HERNANDEZ.)

DEAN HERNANDEZ. Consciousness and awakening–

SHELBY. Right, right, sure, I mean God knows we need to hear that now. But, but, it's like a dollar short and a day late right? You're talking like we live in the clouds. You're writing *books* but no one reads anymore, we're on our phones so…

(SHELBY *holds up her phone.*)

DEAN HERNANDEZ. Cultural and racial renaissance. I write about cultural and racial rebirth–

SHELBY. Well fine but from. Like. Whatever. I don't know. Applying old ways. Just continuing as if the last fifty years didn't happen, it's like living in dust when yeah, maybe a job and an iPhone *is* all each person needs to reach their potential if everyone had one everyone would be informed and be able to vote and so many problems would be solved: access: I mean: you can shoot movies on this thing and it can tell me if I have an ear infection plus keep track of all the shoes I think are cute like Jesus that is amazing that is the kind of world we live in today: *now,* and, and—

(SHELBY *looks at* DEAN HERNANDEZ.)

DEAN HERNANDEZ. Yes, Miss Wilson?

(DEAN HERNANDEZ *looks at* SHELBY.)

SHELBY. This interview isn't going very well, is it?

(DEAN HERNANDEZ *smiles.)*

DEAN HERNANDEZ. I wouldn't say that.
Have Miss Haj schedule for next week. You'll have more questions for me. I'll be more settled in and we can agree to disagree then.

SHELBY. I don't want to disagree. Who wants to disagree? I want, I really need this story for my résumé—

DEAN HERNANDEZ. Miss Haj keeps my book.

(The phone vibrates violently.)

DEAN HERNANDEZ. Pleased to meet you, Miss Wilson.

(DEAN HERNANDEZ *extends a hand to* SHELBY.
SHELBY *looks at* DEAN HERNANDEZ's *hand.)*

SHELBY. Right. Sure.

(The phone vibrates: loud.
The phone vibrates: louder.
As it does, the sound of the dry erase marker begins again.
Squeak, squeak, squeak.
A sweet image appears near the book above: a heart or flower: buoyant. The word "cutie" appears within the heart or flower.)

(The lights change.
Later the same afternoon.
SHELBY *lets out a frustrated growl that turns into a moan.*
A bench.
GRACE *and* SHELBY.
SHELBY's *moan rises.)*

GRACE. I'm sure it wasn't that bad. He said go back next week: go back next week.

SHELBY. It's all arbitrary anyway. Dividing people up. There is one race.

GRACE. That's his whole life's *work,* Shel.

SHELBY. He's an antique, the way he talks about it. And he talks about it *all* the time. On CNN, on NewsHour. I googled him up the wazoo. But if his generation had done its job maybe we could get on with, with. Maybe we wouldn't be seeing the same story over and over in the news. It is the same story, over and over in the news. The world is falling apart.

GRACE. He didn't do that, Shel.

SHELBY. Well, I know—

GRACE. He's been writing about it for years.

SHELBY. *WE HAVE ALL THE BOOKS.*

GRACE. And he is definitely not the one shooting people.

SHELBY. I know that and *you* know what I mean. I just want to write this fucker and be done with it.

GRACE. Basically you told him to go piss on the work he's been doing for those last fifty years—his entire life's work—and flush it down the toilet.

SHELBY. I did not. And he's not that old. Is he?

GRACE. *Go back next week.*

(SHELBY's *phone buzzes.*
SHELBY *picks up her phone and shakes it.)*

SHELBY. What is *wrong* with these *childrens?*

GRACE. You should've applied to the library like me.

SHELBY. They're going to kick me off the paper which cannot happen, just cannot happen—

(SHELBY's *phone buzzes.)*

SHELBY. And these stupid ungrateful freshmen will not stop *calling.* What has it been? Three weeks? Less than a month. Less than a month away from home and they can't live without mommy *whhhhhhhyyyyyyy? Grace:* why is this *happening* to me?

GRACE. Seriously, the library, instead of having four-year-olds as roommates.

SHELBY. That's work-study. I can't. And, RA looks good on paper. And if they were just my roommates they would not be calling me for every little thing that goes wrong all day long.

GRACE. You do get paid for it.

SHELBY. No one normal would do this for free—

(The phone vibrates.
SHELBY *checks it.)*

SHELBY. See? *See?*

GRACE. Just answer it.

SHELBY. They weren't supposed to bother me every frickin' second of the day.

GRACE. Ask to go back to Sherman.

(Beat.)

SHELBY. I don't wanna do that.

GRACE. Doesn't hurt to ask. Sherman, or the library. You don't have to do this all year.

SHELBY. I'm not work-study, I don't qualify for work-study, they're not just going to give me a job.

(Slight shift.)

GRACE. No one just "gave" me a job.

SHELBY. I didn't mean it like that.

GRACE. I work hard.

SHELBY. Um, you sit behind a desk and tell people where the bathroom is.

(Less than a slight shift.)

GRACE. *I am not the one who got fired from the Athletics Department.*

(Beat.)

SHELBY. I didn't.

GRACE. Well no one *gave* me anything, no one is *giving me* anything for free, I am working—hard—to be here.

SHELBY. I know.

GRACE. Yeah, well.

(Silence.
Icy.)

SHELBY. And I didn't get fired.

(GRACE *and* SHELBY *look at each other.*
Something slides, warms.)

SHELBY. Sorry.

(Beat.)

GRACE. Me too.

SHELBY. I know you work. I know that, I do.

(Quiet.
Quiet.
Then.)

GRACE. Just do the interview over. Use that Shelby *je ne sais quoi.*

(The mood rises again.)

SHELBY. I was so nervous I couldn't even work my phone. Me. My phone. GRACE. It was insanity.

GRACE. Shelby, Every Professor loves you.

SHELBY. No every professor loves *you.*

GRACE. No you.

SHELBY. No you.

GRACE. You.

SHELBY. You.

GRACE. Youuuuu.

(They both laugh and giggle hysterically.)

SHELBY. So glad we started that.

(As if they are superheroes or secret agents:)

GRACE. Survival of the freshman onlies. Combating micro-aggression in every class.

SHELBY. "You speak so well."

GRACE. "Could you give us the black perspective?"

SHELBY. "The Japanese[1] perspective?"

GRACE. "Yeah. No I can't 'cause I'm *Korean.*"[2]

---

1 Change from "Japanese" to "Chinese" if actor is Japanese.

2 Change to actor's ethnicity if actor is not Korean American.

SHELBY. "Don't get offended, besides, if you go here you can't complain."

GRACE. "About anything ever."

SHELBY. *Ha.*

GRACE. "Or maybe you don't really *want* to be here?"

SHELBY. Ha.

GRACE. They fucking wish.

(Beat.
SHELBY *groans. Loudly.)*

GRACE. You'll have that dean eating out of the palm of your hand before fall break.

(The phone vibrates.)

SHELBY. They. Are. *Killing.* Me. I have a life force and they are draining it from every bone in my body.

GRACE. Just answer it.

SHELBY. I have a life force and they are draining it from every bone in my body.

*(*SHELBY *looks at her phone.)*

SHELBY. They just want me back at the dorm so I can hold their tiny little hands while they wallow through their own tiny shit.

GRACE. Does Res Life not screen people? You are like the worst resident advisor to walk the face of the earth.

(But GRACE *smiles.*
So SHELBY *smiles, too.)*

SHELBY. That's dramatic.

GRACE. You're dramatic.

SHELBY. My freshmen are dramatic. *I* am realistic.

(The phone vibrates.)

GRACE. Just answer.

SHELBY. There's one kid that wears tighty-whities to the bathroom.

(The phone vibrates.)

GRACE. *Answer your damn phone.*

SHELBY. Like no pants, no robe, just, waltzes down the hall like it's his own personal living room. And another girl, the one who wears these unironic veggie pajamas *every day.* The celery stalks on them have eyes. I think they're following me. She invites people into her room to watch porn on her laptop. I am herding cats.

GRACE. Maybe ask: "What am I afraid of? What am I, Shelby Wilson, when I look into these students' faces, what is it I am running from?"

SHELBY. Thanks psych major.

GRACE. Hey, that's music therapy major to you.

SHELBY. It's all some squishy touchy-feely phssssh that I don't know how you sit through every class. Sports medicine is much more cut and dry.

GRACE. With your hall? You need to ask yourself: how can I change the energy of this situation?

SHELBY. Are you seriously paying for a degree in this subject?

GRACE. They can't all be horrible.

SHELBY. Yes, yes they can. Of course they can. Because of them my interview's going to be late and I'm going to have to go all the way back to Dean Hernandez's office next week all over again.

GRACE. Better read that speech then.

SHELBY. Oh. My. *God.* I *read* it. I do not *agree* with it.

GRACE. Dean Hernandez's just an old hippie. Pretend you're talking to someone who doesn't shower and smokes a lot of weed.

SHELBY. I don't turn things in late, Grace. And, you think he smokes weed?

GRACE. What's your mom say about all this?

SHELBY. How will my mom know if Dean Hernandez smokes weed? You think my *mom* smokes weed?

GRACE. What's your mom say about all this?

SHELBY. She's just going to tell me I told you so about skipping convocation. She's drooling all over Dean Hernandez coming here. I guess she and my dad saw him speak a couple times? I don't know. I am not on board. Content of character, right? Isn't that what they all took and ran with? Then they should use it. It's not right when professors only see us as symbols; it's not right for people like him to make a living off talking about it all over the place either, in this day and age—

GRACE. In this day and age? Are you eighty-five?

(GRACE's *phone vibrates.)*

SHELBY. Oh great, now they're calling *you?*

GRACE. Maybe I have a date.

SHELBY. Yeah right.

GRACE. Rude. There's tons of swipe-right action going on around here.

(GRACE *looks at her phone.)*

GRACE. Whoa.

SHELBY. Is he that ugly?

GRACE. No. *Whoa. Noooooo. Look.*

(GRACE *shows* SHELBY *her phone screen.*
SHELBY *leans in to the phone screen.)*

SHELBY. Whoooоaaaa.

GRACE. Who would do that?

(The sound of the cymbal.
Squeak, squeak, squeak.
The words "Dinner: 6:30: McCougnahey Hall Smiley Face" appear on the dry erase board.)

(The lights change.
Later that same afternoon.
FIONA *and* BRYANT.
The common room on a dormitory hall.
BRYANT *has his phone in hand.)*

FIONA. Dude.

BRYANT. This is off the chain, Fi. All these likes, a hundred shares in like two minutes. The whole campus is like:

(He makes his hands look like something just exploded.)

FIONA. *What* is her *problem?*

BRYANT. Only a matter of time before it's not just all over our campus but like it all spreads–

FIONA. That celery freak posts everything. I should cram her phone down her throat.

BRYANT. It's Alyssa who's pretty upset though. I mean, it's on her door, right. But she's gonna calm down. I mean, once you talk to her.

FIONA. Me? No, no: you. You needa talk to her. Like seriously.

BRYANT. Because why? Because we both black?

FIONA. You know it was a joke, right?

BRYANT. Yeah, sure.

FIONA. Go tell her it was a fucking *joke.* Like afros. Afros are mad funny, when you see them for real on Halloween.

BRYANT. Halloween's not that real, Fi. And, I guess all that on her door was probably shocking?

(FIONA *looks at* BRYANT.
BRYANT *looks at* FIONA.
FIONA *looks away first.)*

FIONA. Call Shelby.

BRYANT. Yeah right. Does this got to do with sprained ankles or Gatorade? That, my friend Fiona, is all Shelby our Surely Stressed RA cares about.

FIONA. This is her job, though. We are *residents* and we need *advising.*

BRYANT. This is some shit.

FIONA. Text her then. *Text* Shelby. I don't answer my phone either but she's gotta see a text, right? Bryant: *Do* it.

BRYANT. Maybe just go talk to her. Talk to Alyssa.

FIONA. I draw all the time. I doodle shit all the time. I have notebooks filled—

BRYANT. With stuff like that?

FIONA. She better not jump off a bridge because of this. My dad will kill me if this turns into some craziness the dean calls home about or some such mess: *damn.*

BRYANT. Alyssa's sensitive, you know that.

FIONA. I do not. I do not know anything about her. What I know about her except now she's about to open her big mouth and get me in trouble. She could do anything, say anything, like in First Year Seminar—

BRYANT. I can't believe that hokey class.

FIONA. First Year Sem she's all up, standing up, talking about stuff she doesn't know anything about, about people she doesn't know anything. She acts like she from the hood, I'd like to know what "hood" she thinks that is. Right?

BRYANT. She was just saying in her *experience*—

FIONA. How she know me? Alyssa don't know me. Telling me about systemic this and that and micro and macro and, and. You know what I say? I say? You know what? Go to where you and me are from, then go to where *she's* from, and *then* tell me who knows what.

BRYANT. There's more to it than that.

FIONA. I better not get kicked out because of her stupid ass. I am so right on this, B, I am *telling* you, Alyssa would not last ten minutes where I'm from. Where you're from either.

(BRYANT *looks at* FIONA.)

BRYANT. ...Maybe.

FIONA. No, I'm right.

BRYANT. I guess I hear that. Shoot, I walk out my front door at home, I got all kinds of people ragging on me.

FIONA. And you got to take it. You got to know how to roll with it. The worst those other kids threw down at me was "snowball."

BRYANT. What the hell's that?

FIONA. That's me, at home. Like now they just call me that all the time. 'Cause when I was little I had this bright white hair—so bright it make a blind man see, right?—and the kids at my school, that's what they'd call me: snowball.

(BRYANT *laughs.)*

BRYANT. That's funny.

FIONA. Fuck you.

BRYANT. That's *funny.*

FIONA. Yeah, it is. See, I can take a joke. Did I go cry like a baby when kids at school yelled that at me? In the halls even. No I sure as shit did not. 'Cause what would they yell back? Those kids would've yelled back "Aw snowball, you melting? You meltin' girl." And then they laugh louder.

BRYANT. Well, there's like a history, a legacy in this country—

FIONA. NO NO NO: my intent was to have a joke. This is complete crapola. Afros are funny. This, this is also *funny.* Go talk to her.

BRYANT. What's in it for me?

(BRYANT *looks at* FIONA.
FIONA *smiles at* BRYANT.
FIONA *kisses* BRYANT.
It's a pretty quick kiss.)

BRYANT. Aww. That was sweet. School-girl sweet. But this is college.

(BRYANT *looks at* FIONA.
FIONA *looks at* BRYANT.
BRYANT *looks at* FIONA.)

BRYANT. In fact, this is a university. They give out PhDs and shit, yo.

(FIONA *laughs.*
BRYANT *grins.)*

FIONA. Oh okay, fine.

(FIONA *cups* BRYANT's *crotch.*
BRYANT *smiles.*
FIONA *kisses* BRYANT *again, with more force.)*

BRYANT. Snowball.

FIONA. You wouldn't know it now. It's almost like yours.

(BRYANT *looks at* FIONA.
BRYANT *pulls away.)*

FIONA. We're almost twins.

BRYANT. Get out of here with that.

FIONA. Don't you think?

BRYANT. You're fine the way you are.

FIONA. No, in the sun, I get dark. I get tan and dark, like you, we'd match, I swear in spring, one good day out in the sun, we'd match.

BRYANT. Whatever you say.

FIONA. We would.

(FIONA *looks at* BRYANT.
BRYANT *and* FIONA *look away from each other.*
Quiet.)

FIONA. At home...I'm...the only white girl to get along with everybody. It's only here no one likes me. My grandparents? bought our house a long time ago? and the neighborhood's? all changed. Everyone my dad grew up with, all those families've moved out but my family's kept the house. It's one way, borrowing against the house, they paid for Catholic school for all of us, so me and my brothers and sisters—'cause there's the seven of us—we were some of the only white kids, but except for snowball no one really picked on me, they knew my brothers would kick the shit out of them. And you know, those families who left? my grandmother would say they would say, when they were packing, they would say to her: "Mary, you stay here, you won't even be able to borrow a cup a sugar no more," 'cause they thought, they just had these ideas the new people would keep to their own, but my grandmother didn't seem to mind a bit. My dad, he– But my grandma. She even's learned some Spanish words 'cause the church changed over about ten years ago? First communion used to be white veils and blonde and red hair. Freckles. Now it's shiny black and brown curls. After a sunburn, I'm almost just as brown as you. I look pretty good.

(Beat.
Beat.)

BRYANT. I'll talk to Alyssa.

FIONA. You'll think I'm amazing.

*(*BRYANT *smiles.*
FIONA *smiles.)*

BRYANT. You kinda…

FIONA. What.

BRYANT. You kinda. You know. Lay it on thick, right?

FIONA. What, you don't like it? What?

*(*FIONA *moves towards* BRYANT.*)*

BRYANT. I do. I like it.

FIONA. Yeah you do.

*(*FIONA *smiles at* BRYANT.
BRYANT *looks at* FIONA.

…

BRYANT *smiles at* FIONA.*)*

FIONA. Talk to Alyssa.

(…

…

BRYANT *blinks.)*

BRYANT. I'll talk to Alyssa.

FIONA. At dinner.

BRYANT. Sure.

FIONA. Talk to her at dinner.

*(*BRYANT *and* FIONA *look at each other.)*

BRYANT. I'll talk to her at dinner.

(BRYANT *and* FIONA *kiss.)*

FIONA. *(Smiling:)* Yeah you will.

(FIONA *leans in to* BRYANT.
Squeak, squeak, squeak.
Giant puckered lips get drawn onto the dry erase board.
When they are completed, we hear a puckering and kiss sound.)

(Early evening.
A cafeteria.
CARSON *enters carrying a tray with an apple on it.*
BRYANT *enters carrying a tray with an apple on it.*
They see each other.
They acknowledge each other.
Friendly.
Other student fill the space.
If the cast is large [i.e. there is the ability to have extra chorus members], others enter the space, too. All carry trays. Each tray has an apple on it.
The sound of the cafeteria turns percussive.
Students mill about. If there are enough students in the chorus, they begin to separate and group themselves according to race and ethnicity: a dance, a ballet with edges. Included are LEIGH, GRACE, RACHEL, BRYANT, FIONA, *and* CARSON. *Absent are* SHELBY *and* ALYSSA. *If there are not enough students to have a fulfilling dance-like experience,* GRACE, RACHEL, BRYANT, FIONA, *and* LEIGH *should mill about the space and regard each other with suspicion.*
BRYANT *and* CARSON *seem distinct from the others, but not bonded as friends.*
Mill, mill, mill: all bite their apples.
BRYANT *and* CARSON *smile faintly at one another.)*

(As the above happens, we see SHELBY *at the bench, looking at her phone, pacing.*
SHELBY *looks at her phone, paces, looks at her phone, paces… paces, paces, paces…)*

BRYANT. Some shit, huh?

CARSON. Oh man yeah. Poor Alyssa.

BRYANT. Like *(He makes a blowing up sound as before).* You seen her? Alyssa?

CARSON. No one's seen her. Her face was like. And then she. No one's seen her at all.

BRYANT. Right.

(Beat.)

BRYANT. Well. If you uh, see her, tell her, I, I, I…

(Beat.)

BRYANT. See you back on the hall, right?

CARSON. Yeah, see you back home, yup.

BRYANT. If the room's a rockin'—

CARSON. What?

BRYANT. I'm just messing with you. I got a quiz tomorrow. Gotta hit the library. I won't even be home 'til late. You got the room to yourself. If you need it?

(CARSON *blinks.)*

BRYANT. Aight, so see you.

CARSON. Oh, okay. Bye.

BRYANT. Later.

CARSON. Bye.

(BRYANT *bites his apple.*
CARSON *bites his apple.*
Both chew.)

(SHELBY *on her phone.*
She also holds a bag of potato chips.)

SHELBY. …*Mom* you are completely and officially *not* helping me with all this: I don't want to go to my hall and I *definitely* do not want to go back to Dean Hernandez's office, I just want to lie in a ditch…I *know* I need this interview and I did *not* get *fired*: *OHMYGODIREADIT*…well no I *don't* know because you and Dad never talk about…I'm not being fresh I…I will turn it *in*: of course I don't want to live in the basement the rest of my life I *wouldn't…* stop yelling—my inner *action*? *I don't know* what my inner action is telling me to do, I am not ten years old anymore Mom…what tone… well maybe if you and Daddy would *tell* me what all that was like I could, I could…because I don't know how to talk, really talk to them and just tell me how to, how to…okay fine, sure, no, I understand, you have to go…I'm not crying, no, no, uh-huh, uh-huh, uh-huh…I'll get it done, I said I'll get it done I will.

(SHELBY *looks at the potato chip bag.)*

SHELBY. Yeah I'm eating great, sure.

(SHELBY *squashes the bag with her hands and stuffs it in her bag.)*

SHELBY. Uh-huh, fine. Love you, too–

(Squeak, squeak, squeak.
Two cartoon-like eyes–vintage, retro: a little bit Betty Boop, and a little bit something else–are drawn on the dry erase board.
The sound of the lips puckering.)

(Later in the evening, but still early.
The common room.)

CARSON. That's some cold-ass shit right there. Just not answering your *phone*. It completely erases our needs, right?

RACHEL. I *knew* this place was whack. When I came on the tour. Brown people in all the pictures online so when you come to visit you think maybe they're all in class but then you sign everything, move in here, and boom. Ha.

LEIGH. *Sucka.*

*(*CARSON *laughs.)*

CARSON. You're so right. The pictures on the website–

RACHEL. I got the real whiff of this place the first week of class. There's a guy sits next to me in Intro to Soc–

LEIGH. Let me guess he's not one of them brown faces in the online pictures.

RACHEL. No, no, *claro que no.*

CARSON. I love it when she speaks Spanish. I love it when you speak–

*(*RACHEL *looks at* CARSON.
RACHEL *starts, then stops, then continues with her original train of thought:)*

RACHEL. This guy in Soc *refuses* to staple, refuses to staple his weekly Reader Responses together in the corner. I said to him, you want to borrow my stapler? He says no, he says, cold day in hell when I staple a paper for this jerk off. I don't think he's ever *ever* had a teacher of color ever.

LEIGH. Intro to Soc is taught by a black person?

RACHEL. I don't know what he is, exactly–

*(*LEIGH *checks her phone.)*

LEIGH. From his campus profile he sure is something.

RACHEL. I didn't think I'd still have to be going to school with people like this. What kind of parents send their kid to college to behave like that?

CARSON. All I know is: I am not, I am no longer, comfortable sleeping here.

LEIGH. If I can sleep here, you can sleep here.

RACHEL. No, Carson's right.

LEIGH. We can *all sleep here.*

CARSON. She's a bully. Fiona? She's a bully.

RACHEL. She's just dumb.

LEIGH. Ummm, dumb can burn your house down, don't get it twisted. Dumb is dangerous.

CARSON. Fiona is a bully and I am not, I am definitely not comfortable.

RACHEL. Fiona, all them down that side of the hall—especially the one with all of Whole Foods painted on her pajamas?— Dumb, dumb, dumb.

LEIGH. I say, I say we take action, right? I say we write the president-of-this-mutha-up-in-here. Go over Shelby's head.

RACHEL. I saw her at convocation, President Verity.

CARSON. Oh I totally slept through that.

RACHEL. Her watch? A buck and a half, easy.

LEIGH. What are you talking about?

CARSON. I did. I knew Fiona was trouble.

RACHEL. President Verity's watch.

CARSON. At orientation, when we all first met, I knew Fiona was trouble. I thought to myself, I thought to myself. Wait, hold up, I know what it is. You know what it is? It's the way she's all over Bryant like he's some exotic pet tiger or something. From minute one, at orientation. She is always rubbing against him—

LEIGH. You're just jealous.

RACHEL. Of which one?

LEIGH. Fiona drapes herself all over him—

CARSON. Like she's a pashmina scarf—

LEIGH. Poor Alyssa.

RACHEL. President Verity's watch is fifteen hundred dollars easy. That is what I am talking about.

LEIGH. Shoot, first black president of this university, she can do whatever she wants, in my book.

RACHEL. Yeah, yeah, yeah but, but if you're picking out fifteen-hundred-dollar watches but your job is, I mean, this is school, this is an institution, of higher fucking learning, this is not Wall Street.

CARSON. I like President Verity. I feel like I could go to her office, have some hot cocoa, get cozy on a chair, just talk.

RACHEL. I like her, too, I like her fine. Before I got here I read all her articles.

CARSON. Black president, black dean—

RACHEL. "Something" soc prof.

LEIGH. Out of um, how many else? Two and a half flies in the buttermilk, that's it. That is it.

CARSON. It's a small school. How many people of color did you expect?

RACHEL. I swear I counted enough Latinos for a student group in that brochure. I look for them in the caf and it's like crickets right?

(She makes a lonely chirping sound.)

CARSON. Well I knew it. I knew Fiona was trouble.

LEIGH. Bryant can't handle himself, that's the problem. Shoot, we're here hardly a month and he's all up in Fiona's business like *Oh* my *good*ness. I mean what is up, right? What kind of brother does that, right? Lets someone roll herself all up on him like that? Where's his sense of self, right? I ask you.

RACHEL. Maybe he's adopted.

CARSON. What's that mean?

LEIGH. No, he's black.

CARSON. Of course he's black.

LEIGH. So you see race or you don't see race?

RACHEL. No one but a Klansman says they do and no, like, he's *black.*

CARSON. Fine, so I'm just the white guy. So I can't say anything right or true about race.

RACHEL. Just admit there are some things you do not know, and listen.

CARSON. Just admit you *attack* and then I do not *feel* like listening.

LEIGH. What Rachel means is culturally, no matter what color tone Bryant's skin is, Bryant is a black person.

CARSON. You act like there's a scale from one to ten. Like a metric system of race—

RACHEL. I wouldn't call it a *scale*. But, like, people, you know, pick up on it. Like I introduce people to my mom and my dad and they look at them and they look at me and my last name's not Spanish but my mom's like basically Sofia Vergara after like six kids and a deep *deep* love of Wendy's chocolate Frostys—

CARSON. That is not nice, Rach.

RACHEL. People see my family and they have no idea where I fall on the Latina scale. Half the time they are calling me Hispanic—which is like whatever sometimes my own family says they're Hispanic—but I am like: am I from *Spain*? I am *Latina*. Go read a Buzzfeed about it or something but do not call me Hispanic because I am not *from Spain*.

LEIGH. What if one of your cousins called themselves Hispanic? What if your own family couldn't agree, present a united front?

RACHEL. I'd lecture whoever that dude is on solidarity until he started to cry or agreed with me. Why? What do you call *your*self?

LEIGH. To me it's the intent, right? You can call me African American, you can call me a name my grandparents fought for, but if your voice is really saying I should be licking your boots, then we got problems.

CARSON. No one asks what I am.

(Both look at CARSON.*)*

CARSON. I hate those boxes on forms. Just an empty space of nothing, which is what "white" means. Those boxes don't tell anyone anything. The whole thing makes me sleepy to think about, it's so...

(Both look at CARSON *but he seems lost in thought and does not elaborate.)*

RACHEL. Me? *I* have my priorities sharpened like a knife. I decide what these people call me. I'm no cartoon to be laughed at. I learned that in high school. You can't serve yourself up to let other people define you.

CARSON. Well I don't use it. I do not use the scale.

RACHEL. Congratulations you are the only one in America who does not notice what the rest of us look like, act like, speak like.

LEIGH. Fiona was, she was trouble from get.

CARSON. Yes, I guess I am. I guess I just maybe am. Maybe I am the last American in the whole states of all the Americas.

(LEIGH *turns to* CARSON.)

LEIGH. Well aren't you the great white heterosexual hegemonic great white hope now, aren't you, Carson?

CARSON. Now you're just being mean. You know, you know, I'm not sure about that whole hetero thing.

RACHEL. Yeah. President Verity's watch is a very, very nice watch.

CARSON. *(To* LEIGH:*)* Take that back.

LEIGH. How'd you get that close to her?

RACHEL. I couldn't see every bit of it, but what I did see, what I did see, made me think: they totally make money off us.

LEIGH. They don't make *shit* off me. I have three scholarships and two loans to be here.

RACHEL. Fine, call up President Verity and tell her what Fiona put on Alyssa's door—and *only* her door, she didn't write that shit on my door, or Carson's door—

LEIGH. I'd like to see her try that shit on my door.

RACHEL. We should call her. See if President Verity comes in here and talks to us in these dorms or sends out a press release first.

LEIGH. President V needs to wake up.

RACHEL. Right?

CARSON. That is some cold-ass *shit,* Shelby not answering her phone. We are *clearly* in need.

LEIGH. Fiona drew it, she should be the one to answer for it.

RACHEL. We're on our own, is what I mean. This place is old. It doesn't matter who's in charge. This place is old and white and it wants to get older—

CARSON. And whiter? Look, every teacher could be black, yellow, and brown, and that would not automatically make it a good school.

RACHEL. This place cannot say it is an institution of higher learning and then just *conveniently* only employ people who all look the same. It cannot and expect to survive.

LEIGH. Shelby and Bryant? People like them got to get themselves together or they got to go.

CARSON. Shelby cares. I think she cares. Which is why I don't get why she is doing this, leaving us alone in here to freakin' freak the freak *out* like this.

LEIGH. Right. She is. Where's Miss Wilson, when you really need her?

CARSON. She spent three hours on the phone with someone's mom last week, I thought she was different–

LEIGH. Miss "I don't see race."

CARSON. Maybe she doesn't. Maybe she is the other real American.

LEIGH. What-the-fuck-ever: I thought I was gonna gag, when she said that at the first hall meeting.

RACHEL. *Everyone does.*

CARSON. I don't. I see two of my best friends.

LEIGH. Awwwwww.

RACHEL. We've known each other for three weeks so, like, whatever.

CARSON. God made the world in seven days, so we've known each other for like three times the Bible.

RACHEL. *Everyone sees race.*

LEIGH. Yeah, you might be on your own for this one, Carson.

RACHEL. Post-racial, post my ass.

LEIGH. Ha.

CARSON. That's very bleak. To say it out loud like that.

RACHEL. You don't see race because you are white, you are the default.

CARSON. We do not live in 1955 Mississippi. It's not 1955 or 1975 or 1985.

RACHEL. Do you even read the newspaper, Carson? You don't even have to look past the front page to get confused about what year it is.

CARSON. If this were 1955 we would not be friends.

LEIGH. Eighth-grade summer, I was washing cars for cheer.

RACHEL. *(Sings:)* Welcome to the car wash: woo-oooo.

CARSON. You're flipped.

LEIGH. I was washing cars for cheer and this car pulls up and it's like one of those old station wagons, huge way-back part, wide as two lanes of the street.

CARSON. *(To* RACHEL*:)* Seriously, what song was that?

LEIGH. And this car, right, it's got this huuuuge billboard strapped to its roof right? And painted on the billboard, like real handwritten paint was "Impeach Obama." And you know, we all, see my neighborhood's, my town is like all black, right? All black people living in the same place for years. It's a historic place. People are proud to come from there. We give house tours at Christmas. Growing up there made me proud to be black. I can't pull out family trees or heirlooms or any of that stuff—how many black families really can?—but my neighborhood makes me fly above all that. But this dude just rolled on into our car wash, with all of us whose parents and grandparents made lives for themselves here, who fought for what power they ended up having, for knowing, whether they agree with Obama or not—I mean, my grandfather hates Obama, but he understands what his presidency means to our neighborhood—it was, I just thought: this is straight-up racist shit here and what makes it, what makes this dude think this is funny, that this is some kind of joke, is we're black girls, the lowest rung of the ladder to him—everywhere in the world just about—and that allows him to pull up and expect us to wash the dirt from his car and "yes sir" him with that sign poking up off his roof with him thinking that Obama sign is a joke. We thought we'd get in trouble, heaps of trouble if we said anything. So we didn't say a word. We washed that dude's car like it was 1955, like it was 1855.

RACHEL. It's always Mississippi, no matter what.

CARSON. No, things change. They do. At home, I have a Chinese grandmother. Me, a white guy, I have a Chinese grandmother. And when I see her I just see my grammie.

RACHEL. Okay I will admit that's sweet.

LEIGH. We like to make racists seem so incredibly evil—like first cousin to the devil—so that it feels like they could never exist, but they do. They exist and they are not the boogeyman. They "just" see your Chinese grammie, too, but the thing is, they see her as "cute" and "adorable" and want to get Chinese recipes from her and act like every word she says should be printed inside a fortune cookie.

CARSON. What is your problem? Why would you say that to me?

LEIGH. Shelby acts like she is living inside a magical fairy world where nothing means anything because she doesn't want it to. I've seen that girl's Facebook page. May as well just post a big dumb yellow smiley face on it 24/7.

CARSON. You're going to judge someone from their Facebook.

LEIGH. Is that not the point of Facebook?

RACHEL. No one real uses Facebook anymore anyway, there's too many parents on there.

LEIGH. There is not one thing on there about Ferguson or Black Lives Matter. Shelby's got nothing on any of that.

RACHEL. Well I don't know. I had to, I know I had to step back from some of all that. Where are the Latinos supposed to fit in all that? Or Native lives? They're dying too?

CARSON. Maybe being political's not her thing.

RACHEL. I am *political,* I am just *conscious* about *how* and that I am *Latina* and race in America is simplified to be black and white but I am not black *or* white—

CARSON. Well maybe she is tired of talking about it. Sometimes people get—

LEIGH. Who has the luxury to just "get tired" of it and "decide" to stop? None of her accounts—Twitter, Etsy—

CARSON. Etsy? So she's supposed to knit about it?

RACHEL. How far back have you trolled her exactly?

LEIGH. I think she turned in her race card, yo. Only thing she wrote about Black Spring was about that mother and her son throwing the brick in Baltimore. And, for the record, my moms would have *beat* my black ass. All she could manage was some shit about violence begetting violence, which is whack.

CARSON. Maybe, Shelby's *evolved beyond* race.

RACHEL. Well race is gonna slap Miss Shelby the RA hard across the face—

LEIGH. Once she walks back on this hall, yes it is.

CARSON. I appreciated her first meeting speech.

LEIGH. Shelby is whack and this *school* is whack *whack* whack: let's all transfer.

CARSON. That's mature.

LEIGH. Everyone sees color.

CARSON. No. No I do not.

LEIGH. Who do you sit with in the caf?

CARSON. Who do *you* sit with in the caf?

RACHEL. I hate that caf.

CARSON. You can sit with me in the caf.

LEIGH. You and Bryant are roommates and you don't even sit with him.

RACHEL. And your grandmother is your "Chinese" grandmother. Not your grandmother.

CARSON. She is *old.* She is from *China.* She is my *CHINESE GRANDMOTHER.*

RACHEL. I say we start posting this outside school, like off campus: blow it the hell up: CNN, HuffPo: *everywhere.*

CARSON. I have a bio quiz tomorrow. Can we time it so it like gets everyone so bothered there's no classes and I don't have to take it? I shouldn't've let my two moms choose my schedule.

LEIGH. Can you imagine if that kid with the brick had *two* black moms? *Shit.*

RACHEL. *(To* CARSON:*)* You cannot *time* a video to go *viral.* That is the *point,* the mob takes over. That is my soc major talking now. I like it.

CARSON. There's a video?

RACHEL. No, there is not a video.

CARSON. I don't want to see Alyssa's face all over the place. Like her face coming home to that.

LEIGH. *There is no video.*

CARSON. She's pretty, Alyssa. It doesn't even look like her, what's up there.

(Beat.)

LEIGH. It doesn't matter what the hell that shit looks like or what Alyssa looks like. What was the *intent,* right?

CARSON. Where the hell'd Fiona know how to draw something like that?

LEIGH. Dumb, dumb, dumb.

CARSON. *I* know that. *I'm* the one who doesn't think we should sleep here. We should camp in the quad.

LEIGH. In the dirt?

RACHEL. That is a genius idea, jerk off.

CARSON. Iamnotthejerkoffyouaretheonessayingmeanthingsabout-mygrammie.

(Beat.)

CARSON. I just don't understand why, why this is happening. Why Fiona'd even do that?

LEIGH. Where the hell could Shelby *be?* What the hell else could she be *doing?* Let's all try again.

(The three take to their phones, text.)

(Squeak, sqeak, squeak.
The dry erase board.
Two bunny ears, cartoonish, get drawn.
Then the words: "Study Break, 8:30" get written, as well.)

*(*LEIGH *types on her phone.*
RACHEL *and* CARSON *pack up their stuff [if they have any] and walk off, texting.*
LEIGH *is left texting.)*

(The bench.
Evening.
SHELBY *sits, book open on her lap.*
The phone vibrates.
The phone beeps.
The phone beeps.
The phone beeps and beeps and beeps.
SHELBY *bites a thumbnail, stares.*
The phone beeps and beeps and beeps.
SHELBY *looks at her phone and places it neatly on her lap.*
SHELBY *sits.*
SHELBY *bites a thumbnail, stares, sighs heavily, gruffly.)*

(Squeak, squeak, squeak.
Leaves and trees appear on the dry erase board.
Foliage.)

*(*GRACE *walks, earbuds in her ears.*
Opposite, RACHEL *walks, earbuds in her ears.*
RACHEL *and* GRACE *bump into each other.)*

GRACE. Sorry.

(They both remove their earbuds and look at each other.)

RACHEL. Oh, I'm sorry.

*(*GRACE *goes to put her earbuds back in.)*

RACHEL. Oh, wait, you're Shelby's friend.

*(*GRACE *looks at* RACHEL.*)*

RACHEL. I live on her hall.

GRACE. Oooooh. Right.

RACHEL. Rachel.

GRACE. Busy night.

RACHEL. Busy night, yeah.

GRACE. Insane.

RACHEL. You um, you seen Shelby? We've all been—

GRACE. I know.

RACHEL. So you know where she is?

(GRACE *looks at* RACHEL.)

GRACE. That picture's intense—

RACHEL. Don't tell me you're like *protecting* her, like *come ON.*

GRACE. I think she needs to process.

RACHEL. Process?

GRACE. She studies sports medicine, she can't talk her way out of a paper bag.

RACHEL. You think she'd do the same for you?

GRACE. What are you talking about?

RACHEL. She wouldn't.

GRACE. You don't know her.

RACHEL. She would not.

GRACE. I don't think that's true.

RACHEL. She takes.

(GRACE *starts to put her earbuds in.)*

RACHEL. I've seen her in the caf. The moment when you get your tray filled and you turn to the dining hall to find your seat and you feel that pang: where do I belong, where do I go? What's it? Three years? She still looks out in the dining room, when she gets her tray. She finds you second.

GRACE. Yeah. Who do you sit with in the caf?

RACHEL. I hate that fucking caf. I fought so hard in high school just to be me and now, here, I have to— I had this teacher, senior year, everything I did. One day I had this orange, I was about to eat this orange, my nail is about to slice into this orange and she yells out "*Rachel,* this is not the time to *eat*" and my face gets hot, although I should have been used to it by then because she was always yelling at me, but, so, I put my orange away but she does not stop, she pulls out her lunch bag and says, "*This* is real food, *Rachel*" and she pulls out crackers and I'm like what the? And she keeps going "This is a *sandwich*" and I think, okay, she is having one of those moments teachers do when they go off and lose it and I get quiet, and the two white girls eating Chips Ahoy in the back keep eating *their* food and I let it go because that's what my mother and father would want me to do, don't make waves, definitely don't act too Spanish, and it's not until the end of the year…I got into here, and this other girl, Mary Ellen Peterson, got rejected from Brown, and she's mouthing off about it during class and saying it's because of students like me she didn't get in, meaning minority students, and that's why, because of quotas and affirmative action, and I could see this teacher suddenly see, that for the entire time she'd been talking to me a certain way and the other students were, were, but the one thing that was not wrong with me, that she could not deny, was my grades, I got As, and so she could not, Mary Ellen could not say these things, and she stopped her, she said, "Mary Ellen, Rachel is not the reason why you did not get into Brown." And it was the first time she saw me, saw the classroom we'd all been sitting in, that she'd created, oranges and sandwiches—all of it—all year. I still would not trust her as far as I could throw her, but I will never forget seeing her see that for herself. As her. Ask Shelby what she sees, when she sees you.

(GRACE *looks at* RACHEL.)

GRACE. At home for myself I'm just Grace. I am not just Asian. I am just me. I came here and thousands of years of world history gets poured into my skin like lava.

RACHEL. Ask her.

GRACE. She's my best friend.

RACHEL. She needs to wake up.

(RACHEL *looks at* GRACE.
GRACE *looks at* RACHEL.)

RACHEL. Next time you see her. Ask her what she sees.

(Quiet.
SHELBY *at the bench.*
SHELBY *stuffs chips into her mouth by the fistful.*
When she's had enough—which is a lot—she stops.
SHELBY *wipes her mouth with the back of her hand, gruffly.*
Beat.
SHELBY *paces some more.)*

(The common room.
LEIGH.
Evening.
BRYANT *enters.)*

BRYANT. 'S'up Leigh-high. You see Alyssa?

LEIGH. She inviting you to Thanksgiving?

BRYANT. It's September.

LEIGH. Your new girlfriend.

BRYANT. We ain't like that, me and Fi.

LEIGH. How could you even talk to her after what she did?

BRYANT. That's why I needa find Alyssa. Smooth this all over.

LEIGH. Whatever, Jeeves.

BRYANT. *What* is your *problem,* Leigh?

LEIGH. How could you even talk to her?

BRYANT. It was a joke, right?

LEIGH. Tell me how it's funny.

BRYANT. Alyssa's always got her books out–

LEIGH. Um, 'cause this is college, right?

BRYANT. You know what I mean.

LEIGH. Good luck with that, government major without books.

BRYANT. All my materials're online, baby: no books, no mess. I travel light.

*(*LEIGH *looks at* BRYANT.*)*

BRYANT. You know where Alyssa is or not?

LEIGH. What's like your deal?

BRYANT. What you mean?

LEIGH. Do you um hate *all* black people or just me and Alyssa? Rachel for good measure? Maybe we throw in Carson too at the end of the day, I hear he's got a Chinese grandma, you could hate her, too.

BRYANT. I don't hate nobody? I'm trying to *find* Alyssa. I'm like an episode of *Cops* up in here.

LEIGH. You got a whole lot of self-hate, that's what you got.

*(*LEIGH *turns to go.)*

BRYANT. Hold up, hold up, hold up—

LEIGH. Why do you even like her? Fiona. Why do you even like her? Why do you keep defending her?

BRYANT. Who cares who I like, do you know where Alyssa is?

LEIGH. Fiona's disgusting. She is a disgusting human being.

BRYANT. You oughta get along with her. Four more years.

LEIGH. I'm lucky it's a huge major. I can avoid that hot buttered mess. Which you should, too.

BRYANT. You know, I don't need this. I'll find her myself.

(BRYANT *goes to leave.)*

LEIGH. Wait. Seriously. For real.

BRYANT. What.

LEIGH. Why?

(BRYANT *stops, looks at* LEIGH.
LEIGH *looks at* BRYANT.
BRYANT *looks down.)*

LEIGH. Alyssa's just as pretty.

BRYANT. She's all right.

LEIGH. Alyssa's just as pretty.

BRYANT. I know. She is.

LEIGH. So why not choose her?

BRYANT. I don't know what she told you, right. I don't know what you girls talked about, but—

LEIGH. And now, after she put that thing up—

BRYANT. It was a *joke.*

LEIGH. What is wrong with you? One girl one time throws herself at you and you're so thirsty you don't even *think,* you don't even *question—*

BRYANT. I get it, you don't like it 'cause of the black girl white girl history thing—

LEIGH. No, no—

BRYANT. You need to get yourself over that, Leigh.

(LEIGH *looks at* BRYANT.)

LEIGH. She is, she is going to take you to Thanksgiving dinner. You're going to sit there at her table and you're going to pass the potatoes and the gravy and the dinner rolls and you're going to sit in front of the television with her father and her uncles and her brothers and you're all going to pretend they are happy to see you and they're going to talk about the football game on TV and you're going to talk about the football game on TV and in the kitchen her mother is going to pull her aside and say it's not me, it's your father and after dessert, when you're helping the aunts clear the table, when you're drying their plates and their cups and their spoons, her dad is going to have a smoke with her on the porch and he's going to finally look at her for the first time since she put on a training bra and he is going to talk to her for the first time since she quit the soccer team and she won't call on Friday and she won't call on Sunday and before finals she'll be through with you because she won't need you anymore. You are so tiny. You are so, so small like a speck.

(Beat.)

BRYANT. Why do you even think about this stuff?

LEIGH. That first day, you *liked* Alyssa.

BRYANT. I carried up a suitcase I didn't propose motherfucking marriage.

LEIGH. She likes you.

BRYANT. We've been here three weeks, who, like, who even knows anything?

LEIGH. You know enough not to be smoothing things over for a fucking disgusting person who by the way is not funny, who by the way is dumb as a bag of bricks if she thought drawing that shit—that "jungle boogie" crap splashed all over Alyssa's bedroom door—if she thought any of that shit was at all funny.

BRYANT. I'll find Alyssa myself.

LEIGH. Yeah? Good luck.

*(*BRYANT *goes to leave.)*

BRYANT. She sees me. Fiona. She likes me. Alyssa. Doesn't act like she sees me, likes me, she. It's harder. I don't know why. With people like Fiona—

LEIGH. White people.

BRYANT. I show up, they're happy to see me.

LEIGH. That's because you put on a show.

BRYANT. When? When I do that?

LEIGH. If I have to tell you, if I have to spell it out–

BRYANT. Maybe I just don't believe in rubbing people the wrong way every single minute of every single day. Not everything is a civil rights thing.

LEIGH. Little tap dance here, little shuffle there.

BRYANT. See, this is, this…

LEIGH. I'm wondering, I'm wondering, when you're going to stop and think on it, like really have to think on it.

(BRYANT *looks at her.)*

BRYANT. I got aunts and uncles and cousins and we're just black. No one goes *around thinking* on it at all.

LEIGH. "And we so happy massa."

BRYANT. We *are.* I don't like feeling like shit all the time so I sit myself in the middle of people who aren't gonna make me feel that way all the time. White people? They don't want to talk about race, they don't want to feel like shit. Most of them, you talk about race, and they out the door fast. With them, it's easier. With you I feel heavy. All the time. I feel exhausted. I don't like it. I should get to choose how I feel, what I feel, when I feel it.

(LEIGH *looks at* BRYANT.
BRYANT *looks at* LEIGH.*)*

BRYANT. But I'd like to talk to Alyssa. Just to say–

LEIGH. Save me some turkey and cranberry sauce.

*(Beep, beep…
The sound of a phone beeping.)*

(The bench.
SHELBY *looks at her phone.*
SHELBY *slumps on the bench like a rag doll.)*

(CARSON *and* FIONA.
The dorm.
CARSON *and* FIONA *pass each other in the hallway.*
They regard each other.
CARSON *seems to linger and they brush by each other.*
CARSON *stops.*
FIONA *stops.)*

FIONA. What do you want?

CARSON. Like, um. Yeah. Like things really, things really've. Hit the.

FIONA. Don't act like you haven't been talking about me all afternoon like some sort of—

CARSON. I just meant there's a lot of tension—

FIONA. I'm not into that new age crapola granola like your moms shoved up your ass your whole life—

CARSON. Okay, like whoa.

FIONA. Don't act like you're on my side.

CARSON. I am not on any *side*—

FIONA. Shyeah, save it for your therapist.

CARSON. What is the matter with you? And who is the one who needs a therapist, climbing into some dude's bed the first week of freshman year like hello? Attention much? Start acting like the engineering major you said you were at orientation.

FIONA. The TAs treat me like shit I think 'cause I'm a girl and it.was.a.*joke*.

CARSON. Well I mean you *drew* it. Does it look funny?

FIONA. My dad has tons of pictures like that in a box in his closet. Obviously someone thinks they're funny or they wouldn't make them.

CARSON. "In a box in his closest" sounds like some shady-ass shit, Fi. Like what is up with your dad?

FIONA. Nothing. Nothing is up with my dad. I just found them. He just has them. Some of them even look a little like Mickey Mouse. Old school. What's wrong with Mickey Mouse? No wonder your major is undeclared you're confused as hell. There is nothing wrong with Mickey Mouse.

CARSON. That shit does not look like Mickey Mouse.

FIONA. They can't take a joke. Back home, the people in my neighborhood, I bet they would've thought it was funny.

CARSON. It's racist.

FIONA. I am not racist.

CARSON. That's not some Disney, shit, Fiona.

FIONA. And you all don't know. I draw all the time. All the time.

CARSON. You draw stuff like that all time?

FIONA. Everyone is so touchy, people didn't used to be like this. People need to calm *down*. Obama got elected that proves we are all *okay*. I mean: what more does everybody want? Everyone needs to quit whining when they offended. This is America. Just work hard and quit fucking whining. There's people have it worse. If you hate it here so much fucking leave.

CARSON. Um like whoa.

FIONA. Oh stop it with the bleeding-heart routine.

CARSON. Fiona.

FIONA. There are certain ways to *be*. It has nothing to do with color.

CARSON. What are you talking about?

FIONA. So much complaining: this is a good place.

CARSON. Well sure but.

FIONA. I see it, I see it where I'm from all the time, all the... Be grateful to be here: get a job, learn English, learn it *correctly*, right? Pay for your own groceries and don't have baby mamas or baby daddies, don't drop out of school, don't rap about hos and guns—

CARSON. Because only white people should have guns.

FIONA. That is not what I said.

CARSON. I don't. I do not know what you mean.

FIONA. What minorities do not want to hear is that numbers-wise, they are not in control, so there cannot be equality, so they need to deal. Here, out in the world.

CARSON. They need to deal with being discriminated against.

FIONA. With how things are.

CARSON. In a few years they will not *be* minorities. And your logic, your logic that it is okay to mistreat people, to be a bigot—

FIONA. *I am not.*

CARSON. Because, because statistically you are entitled to be one, is, is. It's not right.

FIONA. Is what? How about some solidarity, here, Carson? Three weeks hanging out with Leigh and Rachel and those two have made you, made you. Which I do not understand. Admit that could be considered funny. Admit that you—

CARSON. I am not admitting anything.

FIONA. I know you do know what I mean. I know you know what I mean about all of this. They can't have it both ways. We're supposed to like them just because they're black? Or their abuela scrubbed floors? Well guess what, my family worked like dogs, too. Guess what? I had not one thing to do with slavery, so why should I be made to talk about it or think about it over and over again it has absolutely nothing to do with me.

CARSON. What you drew on Alyssa's door has *everything* to do with you: you are the one who *drew* it. And. Newsflash, it looks a lot like something that crawled out of slavery's ass to me.

FIONA. Not everything is *racial*. They make it so hard to be around them when they drag race into *every single thing*. It's not always that. Everything is not always one thing. They are always spouting off. When do *I* get to say how *I'm* feeling? I don't.

CARSON. When you do shit like that, it makes it seem obvious what you feel—

FIONA. They get to spout off about all sorts of things, blame people for things.

CARSON. Who is blaming—?

FIONA. My *brother* is a cop. *And* three of my cousins. When do they get to, get to: my brother does *not*, they all do their jobs, and to sit there in class and have Alyssa spout off about, about. My brother could get blown away anytime, anytime: he could never come home again: and half this country wouldn't give a rat's ass.

CARSON. You just shouldn't have done it.

FIONA. I don't have to explain myself.

CARSON. If you just see it from Alyssa's side.

FIONA. I am what I am and I say what I say and what should I do? *Apologize* for myself all the freaking time? Like is this *America?* Is there not *free speech* here?

CARSON. You can say whatever you want but you can't pretend what you do just exists all by itself, that it doesn't hurt people just because you didn't meant it to, and if it does, just um *yes: apologize.*

FIONA. You know exactly what I mean. By everything. Can't you just agree a little? That it's funny?

CARSON. Can't *you* just say you are sorry?

(Beep, beep.
Beep, beep.
The sound of a phone beeping.)

(The bench.
Later the same evening.
SHELBY.
GRACE *enters.)*

GRACE. You can at least pick up for *me,* right?

(Quiet.
Quiet.
Quiet.
Finally:)

SHELBY. There are no mirrors in our house. In my parents' house: there's no mirrors.

*(*GRACE *waits.*
SHELBY *continues.)*

SHELBY. My parents are very big on inner *actions,* on what you *accomplish.* I've been staring at calendars since the day I was born: every square is always filled up. My great-grandfather? He was good at filling them up, too. He made all his money in real estate. It was one way to do business without showing yourself, without people coming face to face with someone. Over the years that is how our family came to exist. We bought more and more through papers and lawyers. We subsisted on money and cars and good schools. Color? Race? Unless it fit on the glossy side of a black history poster, we all just were not going to talk about it.

Dean Hernandez told me, when I was in his office, that we all have history lapping at our insides and I wish I could see that wide, vast sea inside my grandfather. When did he first decide to hide behind bank notes and house deeds? But I can't ask any of them about any of it.

We were told we had to be better, so if anything happened to us, was said to us, it would not sink in too deeply. When it's Kindergarten and someone whispers some ugly thing at first maybe you don't believe it, but then that whisper can grow. That's when what they taught grows, too. *I am better: I am above this.* So there is no need to have a conversation. So you swallow that ugly instead.

I never learned how to talk about any of it.

GRACE. You're a quick study: go back to your floor and try.

SHELBY. You don't understand. Your parents sent you to Korean school. They gave you cultural consciousness—

GRACE. *(Smiles:)* Every Friday and Saturday. Me and three other Grace Kims. *Four* Esther Lees.[3]

SHELBY. *(A whine:)* Tell me what to *dooooo.*

GRACE. You act like you were raised on a rock all alone but you *were not.* You have experiences to draw upon as a *person.* Go have a conversation with these people.

SHELBY. No, no. *You* are *equipped. I* am not *equipped.* You got this way to know yourself. I bet you never asked the tooth fairy to bring you blonde hair. I wrote the tooth fairy and asked her to leave me blonde hair.

(GRACE *looks at* SHELBY.
GRACE *smiles.)*

GRACE. I wrote to Santa for round eyes.

SHELBY. Those assholes didn't bring us shit.

(Quiet.)

GRACE. You see me, right Shel?

SHELBY. Stay with me, Kim.

GRACE. No, I'm not joking. I...I'm... I am asking. When you see me. What do you see?

SHELBY. I can't have you cracking up, too, Grace.

GRACE. No, I'm not joking. I...I'm asking. When you see me. What do you see? Because. You talk about content of character and labels and you seem hell bent on tearing apart Dean Hernandez—

SHELBY. I just don't understand why my parents, who have Martin Luther King and Kennedy on one wall—and those guys stare ahead and never talk to each other in our house, I've noticed—and Malcolm X on a bookshelf somewhere—I do not understand, I am way past realizing, that my parents, who seem to be in love with the civil rights movement, can not have a conversation about racism that, essentially, says more than "racism sucks."

(Beat.
GRACE *focuses.)*

GRACE. When you see me, what do you see? Like, do you see Asian or Grace or just the only other lonely person to talk to our freshman year? Like what do we have in common?

SHELBY. *See? You* **go talk to my floor.** *You* know how to—

3 Change to appropriate school and appropriate common names if applicable.

GRACE. No, no, I am *asking*. You are *taking* from this and I need you to *give* me an answer or at least join me in, in...

SHELBY. I thought you wanted to help me.

(Shift.)

GRACE. You know I almost didn't come back this fall. I almost went to visit my grandparents in Korea.[4] My grandmother loves spas. Loves spas. She came in May and we went to a few, after finals. To relax she said. My mom paid for everything. And it was. It was very relaxing. By the fourth one. Man, I was super relaxed. My grandmother reached over, we were under some hot towel treatment thing, and she touches my jaw, and she says, "So pretty. Prettier if we just take it in, just a little." I wasn't really surprised. In Korea they do this all the time. I go there and I stand out. Everyone can tell I'm American because I look the most Korean. I'm dark. To them I'm fat. I stand way out. But then she didn't stop. She kept going. She had plans for my eyes, my nose. The color of my hair. It wasn't that it *could* happen, it was that at some point, I knew, she and my mom had planned these trips, spa trips, planned out what work to get done. And I almost didn't come back this semester. I almost fell for it. I almost saw what they did. Almost. At home I'm just me. And I'm going to stay that way. But. So. I need to know what you see. Because I'm proud I'm "dark" and "fat" or their version. And if all that is arbitrary to you, then I don't know, Shelby. I don't know what I am to you.

(Buzz.
The phone.)

GRACE. You should go back to your floor. You shouldn't hide.

(GRACE *looks at* SHELBY.
SHELBY *looks at* GRACE.
Buzz.
But SHELBY *just looks at the phone in her hand.)*

GRACE. Pick it up.

(SHELBY *looks at* GRACE.*)*

GRACE. Answer the phone, Shel, wake up: look *around.*

(SHELBY *looks at her phone.)*

GRACE. Right.

(GRACE *leaves.)*

SHELBY. Grace, no, I, I.

---

4 Please change country if Grace's character is not from Korea.

*(*SHELBY *thinks.*
SHELBY *looks at her phone, then resolves to follow* GRACE.*)*

(Squeak, squeak, squeak.
Cartoon-like cleavage, a la Betty Boop gets drawn.
A bar of "Jungle Boogie" by Kool and the Gang plays.
It's short.
Just a spike of sound.
Squeak, squeak, squeak.
The words "FYI Lights Out: Midnight!" appear on the dry erase board.
Sudden.
A spike.)

*(*ALYSSA *in the common room.*
She is typing on her phone.
CARSON *enters.)*

CARSON. Alyssa. Oh sweetie.

*(*ALYSSA *looks up.*
CARSON *goes to her, then stops short.)*

CARSON. It's disgusting. It's just awful, Alyssa, sweetie. It just is. How are you?

*(*ALYSSA *jerks herself away from* CARSON *and makes a deep guttural sound.*
ALYSSA's *shoulders begin to move.*
ALYSSA's *shoulders begin to shake.*
The sound of the cymbal.
Then music low, rising.
Squeak, squeak, squeak.
ALYSSA's *shoulders shake.*
The dry erase board fills in:
Amidst the typical dry erase board images another image appears.
Its eyes and mouth are cartoonish and garish: extra large, bulging.
The lips from before get filled in: larger, larger, until they too are grotesque.
The foliage fills in to appear like a jungle.
The ears fill in to appear like a rabbit as:
ALYSSA *cries without making sound.*
Squeak, squeak.
Musical notes appear on the dry erase board.
The opening riff to "Jungle Boogie" by Kool and the Gang plays.
ALYSSA *cries without making sound.*
CARSON *looks at* ALYSSA.
CARSON *looks at* ALYSSA.

The music rises, rises.
The sound of water lapping, lapping...)

*(*SHELBY *enters.*
FIONA, BRYANT, RACHEL, LEIGH *enter.*
All speak at once: we hear the first few words of each character's monologue overlap several times:)

BRYANT. How about duck and cover?

CARSON. We're from Raleigh, well, Apex—

RACHEL. I'm your hairdresser, your neighbor—

GRACE. Which ultimately doesn't mean shit.

LEIGH. The problem is, the problem is, all this history folds into itself and, and, and—

BRYANT. How about duck and cover?

CARSON. We're from Raleigh, well, Apex—

RACHEL. I'm your hairdresser, your neighbor—

GRACE. Which ultimately doesn't mean shit.

LEIGH. The problem is, the problem is, all this history folds into itself and, and, and—

BRYANT. How about duck and cover?

CARSON. We're from Raleigh, well, Apex—

RACHEL. I'm your hairdresser, your neighbor—

GRACE. Which ultimately doesn't mean shit.

LEIGH. The problem is, the problem is, all this history folds into itself and, and, and—

(Cacophony, cacophony, cacophony as the above repeats and repeats and rises and rises until:
Beat.
Stop.)

(The following is frenetic.)

BRYANT. Stop and frisk. How about duck and cover? I'm five years old, I'm five years old and I'm in the backseat of my mom's car and I'm playing with this airplane, this white, this like space shuttle, tiny, cast iron, got NASA on the side, and I make this space shuttle twist and turn and twist and turn and I don't pay attention, I twist and twist and when my mom stops the car bam, that seat belt, that damn seat belt, is twisted around my five-year-old self and I can't get loose and she's got her bag from work and my sister's backpack and my lunch box and she's pulling and it's getting tighter and my dad's like let me cut it, I'm gonna cut it and my mom's like call 911 and my dad's like hell no but my mom is like now, call it now and he does and they come and *they* cut me out and my parents breathe for the first time in 20 minutes right and they're about to say thank you, officers, thank you, thank you and one cop is nice, pats my head, pats my dad's back, but the other one, his buddy, just lays into my mom and dad, in front of me, just lays into them like it's all their fault and I want to say it was me flying, it was me soaring, it was me, it was me and my parents who were, who are, everything, everything, to me, to my sister and me, they just stood there, they just took it, they did not move, they did not blink and just like that I knew why, I knew, I saw, how that cop saw them, how that cop saw all four of us...I'll know I'm grown, really grown, have power, when I control how I feel, what I feel, when I feel it. That, that is power. That is all I want. I don't think that is very much to ask. Actually.

CARSON. Actually, she is, she is my grandmother. The way my moms tell it Grammie Lin May was the only one—'cause we're from Raleigh, well, Apex, and it's not like the South, it's not at all like the deep, I mean you have to drive a bit to get to farm people but once you do, you... And their families, my mom's family, on the Mead side, they're pretty well known, and when my mom came out. Gram was the only one. I mean Christmas and Easter and all my birthdays, every single one of my birthdays, my christening, my confirmation: my gram was there for all of those. They all three met at church and Gram took care of them and we are a family. Gram stepped into a role, a choice. Which means everything to me. I don't think I could do that. I know I can't do that. I just think of doing that, and I get tired. My major, the crush I have on my Earth Science lab partner: I don't step forward into anything. So Grammie Lin May means everything to me because she didn't have to take two lesbians under her wing in Apex, North Carolina who probably, who, I know maybe were taught not even to see her, to really see someone like Grammie Lin May, I know that: she did not have to do that at all. But she saw them. She stepped into them. She is my grandmother. And she *does* make amazing Chinese food *and* sweet tea *and* barbecue. I am not like Fiona but Leigh, bless her heart, is wrong she is so wrong I do not see color.

RACHEL. I sure as hell do. My mother? She is. She is like a cartoon. The nails, the lips, the hair: she gets it blown out, her hair. I had no idea it was so curly until I overheard one of my aunt's at Christmas, talk about it. My aunt married a Colombian. A good kind of Latino. My other aunt, married a Mexican. Not a good kind. The aunties make jokes about it. Spins my blood. We learned, my brothers and sister, we learned to pretend to laugh or not say anything at all. The saving grace about my girlfriend to my family is that 1) she goes to Wellesley and 2) she's the good kind: Venezuelan. I see my mother and I see how she serves up this way to be Latina and it changes depending on how many white people are around, how many black people are around, how many Latina people are around. She almost threw a tantrum when, when we went to an Ethiopian restaurant and she noticed our table was where the other Ethiopian people were seated and she went full on white lady—she may as well have been wearing white gloves and a Jackie-O pillbox hat—and demanded a new table. She thought she was being judged for, for, I don't know, the one-tenth of whatever blood no one likes to talk about she has. I am very specific about who I am. I am not my mother. In the movies you do not see me, you see people like my mother. You know her. She's fun and loud. Wears an apron. You don't see people like my kind in the movies. But I am your neighbor, I am your hairdresser, I am your doctor: I am real.

GRACE. Which ultimately, ultimately doesn't mean shit, right? What you say you think, what you want to say you do, what matters is, what matters is: if you can't look someone in the eye and see them, really see them, and then meet them, really meet them—

LEIGH. The problem is, the problem is, all this history, all this history folds into itself and over itself and there's all these lines, all these lines, and it *is* black and white, it *is* here and there, right and wrong you do not, you do not—

FIONA. *And it was a joke.*

CARSON. A black man walks into a bar.

RACHEL. A blonde chick walks into a bar.

BRYANT. A spic walks into a bar.

LEIGH. An Eskimo walks into a bar.

GRACE. A spook.

LEIGH. A cracker.

CARSON. A chink.

RACHEL. A wop.

BRYANT. A jap.

LEIGH. A mick.

GRACE. A kike.

CARSON. Whitetrash.

RACHEL. Indian-giver.

BRYANT. Gook.

LEIGH. Wetback.

GRACE. Guido.

FIONA. A joke.

(Shift.)

BRYANT. You got to ask yourself.

CARSON. Ask yourself.

LEIGH. Ask yourself.

BRYANT. What is a joke?

RACHEL. What's the etymology of a joke?

GRACE. Why do we laugh?

LEIGH. Why do we laugh?

FIONA. We're all *supposed to laugh.*

BRYANT. The magic of a joke.

LEIGH. The kick.

CARSON. Is in.

LEIGH. Is in.

BRYANT. The discovery, right? The joke really happens in the part, at the end, in the picture that's left over. We laugh—

CARSON. We laugh—

GRACE. We laugh.

FIONA. We do, we do laugh—

BRYANT. At different things because we have different thresholds, different, different, thresholds for what is funny or painful or, or—

FIONA. No, no, no—

BRYANT. Americans? Across the board: what do we have in common? We like our jokes aggressive.

CARSON. Bryant, where you from?

BRYANT. I'm from where we don't end sentences with prepositions.

RACHEL. Bryant, where you from, asshole?

FIONA. We can laugh together, see, we laugh together.

(Shift.)

CARSON. Sand nigger.

RACHEL. Prairie nigger.

LEIGH. House nigger.

BRYANT. Field nigger.

CARSON. Nigger nigger.

GRACE. In school it was: ching chong, ching chong.

RACHEL. It was: you're Spanish? Are you legal?

BRYANT. It was: give that kid a football.

LEIGH. It was: but where are you *from*?

GRACE. It was: I love Chinese food can you teach me to make Chinese food? Even though—

RACHEL. You all have the same father?

GRACE. Even though—

LEIGH. Where are you *from*?

GRACE. Even though—

BRYANT. Etymology, right? Where's it come from, right?

GRACE. Chinese, Korean whatever, they're all the same so—

CARSON. I got tan: *we're twins.*

BRYANT. It was: you know how to rap, right?

GRACE. Ching chong ching chong.

LEIGH. This black girl walks into a bar.

ALYSSA. I have a voice.

(Stop.
Stop. Stop. Stop.)

ALYSSA. I took the SATs and I did track and field and I volunteered and I, I, I did all the things, the same things, I think, everyone does. To get here and looking at that door, my bedroom door, seeing how she saw me, if only for a moment, split moment...you think you'll throw down, you think you'll get into it, scratch out eyes, gnash teeth, go for a throat, tear skin and hair. But I just felt exhausted. Bone tired. And bare to the world. Years of history boiling up into this moment, split moment, for everyone to see, a thousand fold. If I could burrow deep, deep, deep...nowhere dark and warm enough to hide me, hide that, if that's what someone could see in me. You think you'll yell and shout, but. I took the SATs and I did track and field and I sat in this food pantry and did the inventory and handed out groceries and families would come in each week and we'd talk and when I got accepted here they were proud of me. Didn't know me or my family before I started helping there and they were proud of me. And in that moment, that split moment, I was so ashamed, of something I know I didn't even do. Stupid. I know it's incredibly stupid. I should have forced, forced air up through my throat, over my tongue to say, to say: there is no maybe, I did everything everyone else did to be here. I am not saying I deserve anything more, I am saying I have a name. I am asking someone to remember my name not look me in the eye and smile and, and, and, erase, erase what I am… I, *I Have A Voice.*

(Shift.)

FIONA. *IT WAS A JOKE.*

(The sound of the cymbal.
The montage stops.)

LEIGH. Like hell it was.

*(*ALL *look at* LEIGH.*)*

SHELBY. Let's all, let's all just—

FIONA. It's not, it is not, my fault Alyssa can't take a fucking joke.

CARSON. Maybe let's make a circle—

*(*SHELBY *looks to* GRACE.*)*

SHELBY. Please Grace. Please. You know how to do this.

*(*GRACE *looks at* SHELBY.
GRACE *looks at* SHELBY.*)*

GRACE. … …A healing circle—

SHELBY. Okay, sure, yes. A healing circle.

LEIGH. I am not making a freaking healing circle.

BRYANT. Yeah, the ship's out to sea on this one, yo.

SHELBY. No, no, we can— If we all calm—

LEIGH. Where the hell have you been?

SHELBY. I, I—

CARSON. She's here now.

SHELBY. Right. We.

LEIGH. There is no we, Miss Post-Racial USA.

SHELBY. I do not believe in labels. There should not be labe—

GRACE. *Shel,* maybe not now.

SHELBY. *I don't.*

GRACE. Just.

SHELBY. Fine.

GRACE. Okay.

(SHELBY *looks at* GRACE.
GRACE *looks at* SHELBY.)

SHELBY. I got this.

GRACE. Sure.

CARSON. Sure. You do. Of course you do. Shelby, you do. Let's let Shelby talk.

LEIGH. No, no, let's not let Shelby do anything. I say we let this motherfucker blow the hell up.

RACHEL. Yeah, I say burn it down. What do you say, Grace?

GRACE. No, let's take some time—

SHELBY. Yes, some time to—

LEIGH. We've given you time enough.

RACHEL. We've given you all night.

SHELBY. I admit. I didn't know—

CARSON. Isn't this your job?

GRACE. Let's air both sides.

LEIGH. There is no "both sides."

SHELBY. Alyssa—

LEIGH. Don't talk to her. *We're* the ones that keep texting, calling.

SHELBY. Well maybe let's let Alyssa.

LEIGH. No, no, do not talk to her. Let's talk to *you, you* who deep down hates, I mean really *loathes* who she is.

SHELBY. I don't.

LEIGH. You can't stand where you came from, who you are, who we are.

SHELBY. That isn't true.

(LEIGH *turns to* GRACE.)

RACHEL. I don't know how you stand her she can barely stand *you*. It's like I said. She doesn't *see* you.

(SHELBY *turns to* GRACE.)

SHELBY. Don't listen to her.

(SHELBY *turns to* LEIGH.)

SHELBY. Let's talk to *Alyssa*—

LEIGH. No, no, *you* talk to *us*. *We* are they ones who've been calling your sorry ass—

FIONA. Like babies. Like little fucking crybabies. People called me snowball and did I cry in my sleeve no I did not. If it was such a big deal, if it was so wrong, Bryant wouldn't be cool with it, he sees it's a joke, don't you Bryant?

SHELBY. Let's all—

FIONA. B.

(BRYANT *looks at* FIONA.
BRYANT *looks at* ALYSSA.
BRYANT *looks at* LEIGH.)

FIONA. You lousy piece of—

LEIGH. Because he's tired of being used—

FIONA. No—

LEIGH. —Of you draping yourself all over him, like he's some circus animal you're parading around and then you won't even talk to me or 'Lyssa or Rachel. We're the only two girls in our major, you won't even look me in the eye—

(FIONA *turns to* BRYANT.)

FIONA. I *like* you—

LEIGH. You like the *idea* of him being black.

FIONA. So I like him being black and I hate you being black, that makes perfect sense.

RACHEL. You don't understand because you don't *listen*.

FIONA. *(To* BRYANT:*)* I like you and you like me. Tell them.

(BRYANT *looks at* FIONA.)

GRACE. Let's try talking this—

FIONA. Bryant. Tell them. And Lys, you know it was a joke—

(CARSON *puts out his hands, waves them as if to say "noooo," to* FIONA.)

CARSON. Shhhhhhh.

FIONA. You were there. You were laughing, too. And this isn't our problem this is their problem. They can't take a lousy joke. You were laughing too, just admit it.

(ALL *look at* CARSON.
CARSON *looks at everybody.*)

CARSON. I shouldn't've. I don't know why I did. I shouldn't've at all.

RACHEL. I knew it, I knew it: you have no point of view, you have the *privilege*—

FIONA. I can't believe this shit. Half of you all were there why are you doing this to me?

GRACE. Maybe if we all take one turn to really get this off our minds, to really—

FIONA. Bryant, tell them. You like me.

BRYANT. I…I…I'm powerful. When I'm with you. Because you need me to be a certain type of…but…it doesn't feel very good.

FIONA. You tell them my *intent*, right?

(BRYANT *looks at* FIONA.)

FIONA. *B.*

(…
…)

BRYANT. I can't.

(FIONA *lunges for* BRYANT.
CARSON *and* RACHEL *stop her.*
SHELBY *lets out a wail.*)

SHELBY. *Ahhhhhhhhh stoooooooop.*

GRACE. Maybe take a deep—

SHELBY. No, no, no.

GRACE. Shel—

SHELBY. It is so easy, it is so easy for you.

GRACE. Shel—

SHELBY. *I never had Korean school.*

LEIGH. Um, you're *black?*

GRACE. Would you stop negating my, my, my experience?

SHELBY. What, Grace, no—

GRACE. Yeah, I get it, life sucks. But you do not have it worse because you are black and you certainly need to learn to *see* people.

SHELBY. I did not say—

GRACE. There is not, there should not be, this, this, pillar, this ladder of, of, racial, race, racial—

SHELBY. We are in this together—

GRACE. You don't act like it.

SHELBY. We are in this—

GRACE. Whatever I say you one up it.

SHELBY. The entire campus is blowing up because of *me,* because of my—

GRACE. At some point you have to listen and take everything in and really, and really, *accept* it and *absorb* and listen—

SHELBY. Oh my God, I can *not* with this shit. You know why? Because I am a sports medicine major. I am not, I do not. We are post-racial, people, we are post-racial I should not be dealing with this crazy shit I should be taking multiple choice *tests* tests about bones and blood and tissue and sinew. Kill each other, go on and rip each other to shreds I do not care: *I DO NOT CARE.* You're behaving like animals, like, like, you're trying to rise up and above but instead you're just biting and clawing each other and this is exactly what, this is exactly what...race is a *distraction,* it is, it is this made up thing that you all are letting *distract* you from, from. There is so much other stuff, real stuff, I mean these labels are not, are not none of this is real it is silly, it is stupid, it is *as-i-NINE* to get stuck, to get stuck, to get, to be you are all just *stuck* on this *idea* and it is, it is. I am so tired.

(ALL *look at* SHELBY.)

(Dark, dark...but light remains on the dry erase board. Dark then turns to the soft glow of dawn.)

(DEAN HERNANDEZ's *office.*
Morning.
SHELBY *sits.*
DEAN HERNANDEZ *enters.)*

DEAN. Ah, Miss Wilson. Good morning.

SHELBY. You know why I'm here.

DEAN. Miss Haj told me you've been waiting.

SHELBY. I needed to come now, not next week.

DEAN HERNANDEZ. It seems the campus has seen quite the night.

SHELBY. They're all revolting. Even my best friend will probably never speak to me again. It's. A mess—

DEAN HERNANDEZ. Can I get you some tea?

(SHELBY *smirks.)*

SHELBY. Is that what you made the Black Panthers to drink when the shit hit the fan?

(DEAN HERNANDEZ *grins.)*

DEAN HERNANDEZ. I don't think you did your homework, Miss Wilson. I was a just an "associate" of the Panthers.

SHELBY. So no tea?

DEAN HERNANDEZ. But I found their social outreach programs very exciting, energizing. A child cannot learn if she is hungry. A person won't ask for change if he's too busy worrying about food and shelter. I hope you read up on that part, too, Miss Wilson. Most people go for the sensational material and don't attend to the basics.

SHELBY. You like that word: *attend.*

DEAN HERNANDEZ. I do.

(Quiet.
Quiet.
SHELBY *slumps.)*

SHELBY. It's me. It's all my fault. All of this—

DEAN HERNANDEZ. Surely this is not so, Miss Wilson. I'll get you that tea.

SHELBY. I came here to help put people back together. My major? Sports medicine? That's all I came here for.

DEAN HERNANDEZ. Admirable.

SHELBY. No. It isn't. I didn't want to get messy.

DEAN HERNANDEZ. I see.

SHELBY. Keeping ice packs cold, putting clean towels by the whirlpool. Last year, that was my job. But I got fired. See there was this player, a five-year player. Fills up a seat on the bench so the team is deep, but is a little too small or too slow or too dumb to really play and he'd busted up his knee in a practice and was out, kaput, done. I got to know him when he'd stand in the whirlpool for the heat. I'm just here to play ball, he'd say, I'm going to get better and play more ball. Never a star, always a team player, and my job was to record his progress and my boss was all over me to get it all down so they could kick him off the team, but football was his *life,* he'd been playing since he was five years old. A few scribbles on my sheets and it was all going to end. So I...I didn't take down everything the way I should've. I let myself get messy. I let myself get messy because that kid is the only other black kid in my year. Because before I worked at Sherman I did not cause trouble, I did not draw attention to myself. In my family you do not let anyone see how scared you are, even if you're shaking so bad you can hardly stand up. And you sure as hell do not let anyone see the parts of you that are different. But I sat with that ball player and I know, I know I saw him and he saw me and I wasn't going to let this school—this place that just a few years ago wouldn't've let us in if we'd paid it—I was not going to let them kick him out, I wasn't going to let them erase him. I kept that kid on that team until my boss found out and: no more job. Big hole on my resume. My parents, my *mom* was *pissed.* Your story, becoming editor, was supposed to fill it up. But I do not like muck and mess. It's much better to keep your nose clean.

DEAN HERNANDEZ. Well that's unfortunate 'cause seems to me like your nose is deep in it, Miss Wilson.

SHELBY. Tell me what should come next.

(SHELBY *looks at* DEAN HERNANDEZ.)

SHELBY. Please.

DEAN HERNANDEZ. Make something of the mess. Just 'cause you're sitting looking at a heap of junk doesn't mean it has to stay that way.

SHELBY. You and my parents' generation were supposed to bring the change up in here.

DEAN HERNANDEZ. Wade around in the muck. See what happens.

SHELBY. I hear "shut it down" and I don't even know what that means. Shut down what? Go back to living in tents and mud huts? Mike Brown, Trayvon, Tamir Rice, Freddie Gray, Sandra Bland—

DEAN HERNANDEZ. Those names slip over and off your tongue so, so easily Miss Wilson.

(SHELBY *looks at* DEAN HERNANDEZ.)

SHELBY. Those are sad stories. They are terrible things.

DEAN HERNANDEZ. The history—

SHELBY. I know the history.

DEAN HERNANDEZ. And yet. Those names slip over and off your tongue so, so easily.

SHELBY. I know the history. I know it. I do.

DEAN HERNANDEZ. But you don't own it.

SHELBY. Of course I don't own it. I'm not the one who did those things and I'm not the one who should—

DEAN HERNANDEZ. Miss Wilson you conduct yourself as if perhaps you really do not know very much history at all.

SHELBY. My history is Power Rangers and SpongeBob. My worldview is a bunch of memes cut and pasted together. My history will be, when I look back: why sit and talk to someone when I can just look it up and know the answer for myself, by myself.

DEAN HERNANDEZ. I'll get that tea. Send you on your way—

SHELBY. My generation is going to evade history. I think we are going to do that and there's nothing you and my parents can do about it and you have no answers to that and you all can't stand that. You're asking us to answer old dead questions. The world we're going to live in does not even exist yet.

DEAN HERNANDEZ. And yet, here we are. Paralyzed by it. Because, on the contrary, Miss Wilson, history defines everything. It outlines, it highlights, it labels: everything. It is the alpha and the omega—

SHELBY. This kind of thing, this kind of talk drives me crazy, your convocation speech—

DEAN HERNANDEZ. We do not need to agree, of course we do not need to agree, but we do need to acknowledge, we do need to admit, that what is in that picture is soaked through in history, it is soaked through with a message that is now splattered all over that girl and that picture did not just appear there, Miss Wilson, someone, some one person thought it and drew it and whether she understands it or not, history has leaked out and made messes all over the place whether you like it or not. You can choose to believe in the tooth fairy, Miss Wilson. You cannot choose whether or not to believe in history. You have the ability to reshape all this mess. You, indeed, own it.

SHELBY. Maybe they'll all just transfer. Let it all blow over.

DEAN HERNANDEZ. They deserve much more than that.

SHELBY. They should not be my problem.

(Quiet.
Quiet.
Quiet.
DEAN HERNANDEZ *considers before he speaks.)*

DEAN HERNANDEZ. Baltimore.

SHELBY. Transfer them all to the same school? Yeah, right.

DEAN HERNANDEZ. I saw the whole of Baltimore from May until December—

*(*DEAN HERNANDEZ *looks at* SHELBY.*)*

DEAN HERNANDEZ. Countee Cullen. Poet.

SHELBY. I knew you were this kind. This kind of professor who tricks students into—

DEAN HERNANDEZ.
I saw the whole of Baltimore from May until December
Of all the things that happen'd there that's all that I remember.

"Incident."

SHELBY. I only took one English.

DEAN HERNANDEZ. Little black boy rides the train, gets called the nasty name little black boys often get called, which I have been called. "Hernandez" is one thing. Black and Hernandez...well, this little boy, that is all he remembers from his trip to Maryland. Not the food or the Bay or, see, when I was little and heard this, read this, I thought of all the aunts and uncles, this kid must have visited with. I thought of Sundays maybe at his grandfather's church, I thought of him sitting on a stoop in July heat. I thought of him hauling out somewhere with a cousin or two to swim, cool off...I felt, Miss Wilson, this little boy was me and I felt, with particular keenness, Miss Wilson, with a sharp, sharp pang in my side and fire in my throat, that moment when Cullen writes and I'm not lying when I say, when I say, that when I read this as a child: a young black kid reading about this ride on this train I knew, I knew, I could see into this boy's eyes. I knew I could *see* him and he could see me. It is not about labels it is about seeing, really, seeing and saying "I see." I see and I agree you have worth.

You do not know this piece of writing, Miss Wilson?

SHELBY. Probably, I guess. I don't know.

DEAN HERNANDEZ. I tell you I was haunted, haunted by this poem where Cullen names, explicitly, what happens to him because of who he is.

(SHELBY *looks at* DEAN HERNANDEZ.)

DEAN HERNANDEZ.
Now I was eight and very small,
And he was no whit bigger
And so I smiled, but he poked out
His tongue, and called me—

SHELBY. *I get it.*

DEAN HERNANDEZ. When you refuse to name it, Miss Wilson, it grows thick and clean and pure and has the power—

SHELBY. I just want you to help me.

(DEAN HERNANDEZ *looks at* SHELBY.
Beat.
Quiet.
Beat.
Quiet.)

DEAN HERNANDEZ. Cullen writes, he writes, that this, this train ride is all he remembers of his trip. I swear I could see him because I knew that, that pin prick when the rest of the suit felt fine, that drop of ice cold rain when the skies seemed so blue and the sun—

(SHELBY *shifts.*)

DEAN HERNANDEZ. This does not have to be their Baltimore, Miss Wilson—something that sits and festers. Sure, this morning I'll call all the appropriate people I should call—the health centers, the other deans, President Verity, the parents. But you don't need to wait for me to do all that.

SHELBY. It's that I don't feel comfortable—

DEAN HERNANDEZ. We're not on this campus to feel comfortable, to bathe in what makes us happy or what makes us feel right and powerful all the time.

SHELBY. I know that—

DEAN HERNANDEZ. Go get your hands dirty.

(SHELBY *looks at* DEAN HERNANDEZ.)

DEAN HERNANDEZ. And make an appointment with Miss Haj. You owe me an interview.

SHELBY. I'm not going to make my deadline. The sun's about to come up. It's way too late.

DEAN HERNANDEZ. Indeed it is. But: you write a new story, how about?

(SHELBY *looks at* DEAN HERNANDEZ.
DEAN HERNANDEZ *smiles at* SHELBY.)

DEAN HERNANDEZ. We do not need to agree but we must try to live in—to *attend*—the same set of conversations while we are here.

(Sound.
All the hallmates speaking at once.
Soft.)

SHELBY. How can I ask them to do that, if I don't know what those conversations are supposed to *be*? For anybody. I don't, I don't.

(The hallmates' speech gets a bit louder.
SHELBY *looks in their direction.)*

DEAN HERNANDEZ. That ball player, you felt for him.

SHELBY. Yeah. I did.

DEAN HERNANDEZ. Whether or not it was wrong you wanted to do right by him.

SHELBY. Yes.

DEAN HERNANDEZ. So there's a voice inside you. Maybe just a whisper of a voice. That wants to try to do right and it's frightening. It's difficult because it's angry and upset—

SHELBY. Yeah.

DEAN HERNANDEZ. But above all: it exists.

SHELBY. It does.

DEAN HERNANDEZ. Don't ignore it. Attend to it.

SHELBY. Attend.

DEAN HERNANDEZ. Attend.

(Voices as before.
The common room.
SHELBY *looks towards the space.*
SHELBY *steps into the space.*

The hallmates and GRACE *are quiet.*
GRACE *looks at* SHELBY.
SHELBY *looks at* GRACE.*)*

SHELBY. *(To* GRACE:*)* I'm sorry. For not listening for...everything. I do. I don't know how to talk about all of it, with every single person—

GRACE. No one does. If they say they do they're bluffing.

SHELBY. But I'm gonna try.

GRACE. Yep.

*(*GRACE *smiles at* SHELBY.
SHELBY *smiles at* GRACE.
[This moment should be sweet but not overly sentimental.
A hug is most likely most definitely too much.]
SHELBY *takes in the group.*
SHELBY *looks at* ALYSSA.
ALYSSA *looks at* SHELBY.*)*

SHELBY. Alyssa, let's start with you.

*(*ALYSSA *looks at them all.*
ALYSSA *takes a step forward.*
As she is about to speak the dry erase boards fills with more marker, which covers up all grotesque imagery from before.
SHELBY *motions for* FIONA *to join.*
The dry erase board fills with more marker: elegant circles and arcs.
One by one all join the circle to talk.
The dry erase board, completely filled begins to erase itself.
The group speaks.
We do not hear their voices.
ALYSSA *is the most animated.*
Evidence of their discussion should suggest it is lively rather than dismal, robust rather than sentimental. It is indeed, a discussion. Not a rally, not therapy. A beginning to the new school year.
The sound of the cymbal, soft.)

End of Play

Also available at Playscripts, Inc.

I and You
by Lauren Gunderson

Drama
90-100 minutes
1 female, 1 male

One afternoon, Anthony arrives unexpectedly at classmate Caroline's door bearing a beat-up copy of Walt Whitman's *Leaves of Grass,* an urgent assignment from their English teacher. Homebound due to illness, Caroline hasn't been to school in months, but she is as quick and sardonic as Anthony is athletic, sensitive, and popular. As these two let down their guards and share their secrets, this seemingly mundane poetry project unlocks a much deeper mystery that has brought them together. *I and You* is an ode to youth, life, love, and the strange beauty of human connectedness.

Good Kids
by Naomi Iizuka

Drama
80-85 minutes
8 female, 4 male

Something happened to Chloe after that party last Saturday night. Something she says she can't remember. Something everybody is talking about. Set at a Midwestern high school, in a world of Facebook and Twitter, smartphones and YouTube, *Good Kids* explores a casual sexual encounter gone wrong and its very public aftermath. Who's telling the truth? Whose version of the story do you believe? And what does that say about you?

Order online at: www.playscripts.com